ROUTLEDGE LIBRARY EDITIONS:
LIBRARY AND INFORMATION SCIENCE

Volume 61

NEWSPAPERS IN THE LIBRARY

NEWSPAPERS IN THE LIBRARY
New Approaches to Management
and Reference Work

Edited by
LOIS N. UPHAM

LONDON AND NEW YORK

First published in 1988 by The Haworth Press, Inc.

This edition first published in 2020
by Routledge
2 Park Square, Milton Park, Abingdon, Oxon OX14 4RN

and by Routledge
52 Vanderbilt Avenue, New York, NY 10017

Routledge is an imprint of the Taylor & Francis Group, an informa business

© 1988 The Haworth Press, Inc.

All rights reserved. No part of this book may be reprinted or reproduced or utilised in any form or by any electronic, mechanical, or other means, now known or hereafter invented, including photocopying and recording, or in any information storage or retrieval system, without permission in writing from the publishers.

Trademark notice: Product or corporate names may be trademarks or registered trademarks, and are used only for identification and explanation without intent to infringe.

British Library Cataloguing in Publication Data
A catalogue record for this book is available from the British Library

ISBN: 978-0-367-34616-4 (Set)
ISBN: 978-0-429-34352-0 (Set) (ebk)
ISBN: 978-0-367-37672-7 (Volume 61) (hbk)
ISBN: 978-0-367-37681-9 (Volume 61) (pbk)
ISBN: 978-0-429-35559-2 (Volume 61) (ebk)

Publisher's Note
The publisher has gone to great lengths to ensure the quality of this reprint but points out that some imperfections in the original copies may be apparent.

Disclaimer
The publisher has made every effort to trace copyright holders and would welcome correspondence from those they have been unable to trace.

Newspapers in the Library: New Approaches to Management and Reference Work

Lois N. Upham
Editor

The Haworth Press
New York • London

Newspapers in the Library: New Approaches to Management and Reference Work is monographic supplement #4 to the journal *The Serials Librarian*. It is not supplied as part of the subscription to the journal, but is available from the publisher at an additional charge.

© 1988 by The Haworth Press, Inc. All rights reserved. No part of this work may be reproduced or utilized in any form or by any means, electronic or mechanical, including photocopying, microfilm and recording, or by any information storage and retrieval system, without permission in writing from the publisher. Printed in the United States of America.

The Haworth Press, Inc., 12 West 32 Street, New York, NY 10001
EUROSPAN/Haworth, 3 Henrietta Street, London WC2E 8LU England

Library of Congress Cataloging-in-Publication Data

Newspapers in the library.

(Monographic supplement #4 to the Serials librarian, volume 14, 1988)
Includes bibliographical references and index.
1. Libraries—Special collections—Newspapers. 2. Newspaper and periodical libraries. 3. Reference services (Libraries)   I. Upham, Lois N.   II. Series: Monographic supplement ... to the Serials librarian; #4.
Z692.N4N48   1988   026 .02517'32   87-29866
ISBN 0-86656-688-0

CONTENTS

Introduction   vii
   Lois N. Upham

Newspapers — Toward Preserving a National Resource   1
   Elaine W. Woods

Creating a Newspaper Bibliography: The Indiana Newspaper Bibliography Project   13
   John W. Miller

Uniform Titles for Newspapers: A Proposal   21
   Lois N. Upham

The Physical Aspects of Newspaper Collection Management: Some Problems and Their Solution   29
   Thomas D. Lund

The Microfilming of Newspapers — The Indiana Historical Society Newspaper Microfilm Project   37
   John W. Miller

Working in a Newspaper Reference Collection   43
   Heidi K. Martin

Newspaper Collections at the Center for Research Libraries   63
   Karla D. Petersen
   Ray Boylan

The Who, What, When, Where, Why and How of a Corporate
    Newspaper Library   71
        Sandra E. Fitzgerald

Education for Newspaper Librarianship   93
    Mary Ellen Soper

There's Gold in Them Thar Reels: Or How Microfilmed
    Newspapers Saved a Region's History   99
        Charles L. Sullivan

Newspapers Can Yield Genealogical Gems:
    One Amateur Genealogist's Experience   109
        Larry L. Murdock

Military Newspapers: A Brief Overview   121
    Robert C. Boots

International Newspaper Considerations   125
    Hana Komorous

A Selective Overview of Newspaper Indexes—1986   133
    Edward D. Starkey

Microcomputer Uses in a State Newspaper Project   143
    Rebecca M. Maier

The Effects of Emerging Technologies on Newspaper Storage
    and Retrieval   153
        J. J. Hayden III

Index   161

Introduction

The impetus for this volume arose from the frustration experienced by the editor during a search for basic information about newspapers in libraries and information centers. Although there are articles and even entire volumes about special libraries that serve newspaper staffs and about the problems of deteriorating newspaper collections (along with companion efforts to preserve them) as well as a scattering of entries in collection development texts alluding to the difficulty of procuring and maintaining newspapers in libraries, no single up-to-date discussion exists of the basic activities associated with newspapers in libraries and information centers. While newspapers are becoming increasingly recognized as an important, indeed unequaled, source of information about current history and local events, they have been largely ignored by information specialists, probably as a result of the very problems discussed in collection development volumes.

Recent activities in the information community have begun to focus upon newspapers and upon their worth to researchers of both professional and amateur status. The most noteworthy of these is the United States Newspaper Project. It was through this project that the editor of this volume experienced new interest in and involvement with newspapers. It was, in fact, at least partly because of the project that the initial search for publications about newspaper use and handling was undertaken. As stated, the search was largely a frustrating one. This volume was undertaken in an attempt to, at least in small measure, fill the lack of general information about this important information source.

This work is intended to be a "sampler" of papers written by individuals who are involved with newspapers on a personal basis. Some work with them in their daily jobs, some use them as tools in their research efforts, others are concerned with them as an ingredient in a larger process. The United States Newspaper Project (USNP), undoubtedly the most significant newspaper-oriented bibliographic activity under way in the U.S. at the current time, is discussed only peripherally in this work. This omission was made possible by publication of issue 6:4 of *Cataloging & Classification Quarterly*. The issue, entitled "The United States Newspaper Program: Cataloging Aspects," did a fine job of covering material that would otherwise have had to be included in this volume. It is recommended that these works be utilized as a set when attempting to achieve an overview of current newspaper handling activity in the U.S.

In formulating the list of contents for a project such as this, a rapid realization is quickly gained that choices have to be made. Even though it became unnecessary to cover in depth the cataloging aspects of the U.S. Newspaper Project, it was still not possible to include a discussion of every problem, dis/advantage, recommendation, etc., concerning newspapers. In keeping with the sampling approach, therefore, articles on both bibliographical and physical control of newspapers are included. Discussions on working with newspaper collections in a variety of settings, viewed from the point of view of both provider and user of information, are also found herein. Consideration of international, educational and technical aspects are likewise included. An overview of activities leading up to the current state of affairs begins the volume.

There will, undoubtedly, be favorite topics that some readers will seek and not find. This "lack," while certainly regrettable, should not detract from the intent of the effort, which is to provide a balanced overview—an introduction if you will—to a variety of topics associated with the use and handling of newspapers in libraries and information centers. It is sincerely hoped that both this work and The United States Newspaper Program volume of *Cataloging & Classification Quarterly* will provide scholars, authors, and researchers with encouragement to continue work on this topic. Not only must information specialists realize that newspapers are an important, although too often forgotten or ignored information resource, but they must be aware that they have a real responsibility to provide access to and protection for this unique category of materials.

Lois N. Upham

Newspapers — Toward Preserving a National Resource

Elaine W. Woods

SUMMARY. Following a brief discussion of past efforts at handling newspapers in an information setting, this article discusses the overall development and progress of the United States Newspaper Project (USNP). The author then goes on to consider a number of major questions that must be answered by the information community if true bibliographic control and preservation of newspapers is to be achieved.

Newspapers constitute one of the country's most important primary research resources for the study of American history and culture. For the professional historian, they are an indispensable source for the reconstruction of state, local or national history. For the sociologist or economist, newspapers contain information on changes in population, social heritage, political outlook, and the economic climate of a region. For the student of local history, they are often the only research source available. For the genealogist researching family histories, newspapers are a primary source for locating birth and death dates and information on marriages.

THE LIBRARY'S PROBLEM CHILD

Despite the tremendous importance, newspapers have until recently been largely neglected by the library profession. There were many reasons for this, most of which concerned the nature of newspapers themselves.

Newspapers are physically difficult to handle. They are both bulky

---

Elaine Woods is a private information systems consultant working in the Washington, D.C. area. She was employed by the Library of Congress for a number of years, where among her many responsibilities she worked on the development of the MARC Serials Format. Under special contract, she assisted in preparing the first edition of the *Newspaper Cataloging Manual*.

and fragile. Their bulk creates both handling problems and costly storage problems. In addition, they are extremely fragile. Newspapers published since 1880 on highly acidic woodpulp disintegrate rapidly, creating the need for expensive microfilming programs to preserve them for posterity.

Establishing bibliographic control over newspapers is difficult. Newspaper publishers frequently adjust masthead styles, and often change the title in doing so. The *Weekly Salina Journal* can become the *Salina Weekly Journal* overnight. Volume and issue numbers, if present, are often assigned capriciously. Until recently, very few libraries cataloged newspapers. In fact, there were no specific newspaper cataloging rules and no generally accepted rules as to how newspaper cataloging should be done.

Guides to newspaper titles and locations on the national level were limited. Major current national directories of newspapers were produced by commercial firms as a means of assessing circulation figures in the fixing of advertising rates. While containing much useful information, these guides did not contain any location information. The three national union lists of newspapers were inadequate in various ways. Gregory's *American Newspapers, 1821-1936*,[1] published in 1937, was out of date, incomplete, unreliable and hard to use; Brigham's *History and Bibliography of American Newspapers, 1690-1820*,[2] contained only newspapers published before 1820; and *Newspapers in Microform*,[3] published by the Library of Congress, was limited to microform copies and based on voluntary reporting by other institutions.

While local efforts to report newspaper titles and holdings existed, such efforts were limited in scope and usually in a non-standard format. Preparation of any union list, regional or national, was highly labor-intensive and printed location tools were often out of date as soon as, if not before, they were printed. Complicating the compilation of any comprehensive location tool was the fact that newspaper holdings are spread throughout many different types of institutions: newspaper offices, state archives, state, public and academic libraries and local courthouses as well as the homes of private collectors.

Access to the contents of newspapers has always been limited. With the exception of the indexes to such national papers as *The New York Times* and *The Wall Street Journal*, most indexes were locally compiled card files, maintained by dedicated individuals. Using newspapers as a reference source usually involved the time-consuming effort of poring through many large, hefty volumes or scanning reels of microfilm.

Given the many problems associated with collecting, handling, locating and accessing newspapers effectively, it is not surprising that few libraries could find the resources to do so. There was much disparity among state programs in handling newspaper holdings. Some states had laws that required newspapers to be held as a matter of public record. While some of these legal deposit collections were in themselves excellent and were housed under ideal conditions, many others were housed in damp courthouse basements or in overheated attics of public buildings. With a few notable exceptions, the general climate was one of benign neglect. A survey of library literature for the last forty years supports this theory. Articles on the handling of newspapers in libraries, with the exception of specialized newspaper libraries, are almost non-existent.

Libraries simply did not have the means, the funds, or until recently the technology to mount a coordinated program to gain control over our nation's newspapers. Clearly, what was needed was a massive national undertaking to locate, describe and preserve this precious national resource.

THE UNITED STATES NEWSPAPER PROGRAM

The United States Newspaper Program (USNP) is the result of a ten-year planning and development effort involving the National Endowment for the Humanities, the Organization of American Historians, the Library of Congress, the Council on Library Resources, and individual historians, librarians, and archivists throughout the country. An interdisciplinary accomplishment, this program is a coordinated national effort to identify, locate and selectively preserve a significant portion of the newspapers published in this country since the seventeenth century. The USNP is an excellent example of cooperation on the part of a user community, the library profession, and the federal government in meeting a national need. Because it can serve as a model for future cooperative efforts, the steps leading to the implementation of this program are significant.

During the 1960s, historians and other researchers increasingly expressed concern about the inadequacy of the guides to newspaper resources. In 1965, representatives of historical associations and historical journals, bibliographers and librarians established a Joint Committee on Bibliographical Services to History. In 1967, this committee sponsored the Belmont Conference, at which the results of a questionnaire citing the deficiencies of Gregory's *American Newspapers* was reported. Following this conference, the Organization of

American Historians pressed for the revision of Gregory, listing this as a high priority item among the needs of American historians.

In 1971, the National Endowment for the Humanities asked the American Council of Learned Societies (ACLS) to provide information that would make "a compelling case" for the establishment by the Endowment of an adequately funded, long-term program for the preparation of important research tools most needed by scholars. The ACLS in turn, queried its constituent societies for projects and the OAH recommended a program to organize, preserve and make available United States newspaper resources.

In 1973, the OAH received a two-year grant from the Endowment to conduct a preliminary survey to determine the need for and problems associated with a complete revision of Gregory's *American Newspapers*. The results of this preliminary study showed (1) that there was a universal need for such a revision; and (2) that working on a state-by-state basis through a single statewide coordinator was the most logical way to proceed with the revision, as a large percentage of newspapers were found only in the state of their origin. Most importantly, this preliminary survey showed what a massive undertaking such a project would be and postulated that libraries would need to play a role in its implementation. The Endowment also perceived that the involvement of libraries was critical to the success of the project and asked that any future proposal should demonstrate involvement by the Library of Congress. The Endowment asked further that any future proposal address itself as well to the need for newspaper preservation.

In 1976 the Endowment funded a proposal in which OAH, joined by the Library of Congress as cosponsor, requested funds for the first phase of a United States Newspaper Project. This grant provided funds (1) to operate a coordinating office at the OAH headquarters during 1976-1977; (2) to implement a two-year pilot project in the state of Iowa to demonstrate the viability of a national program based on individual state projects; and (3) to hold a number of state planning conferences.

Meanwhile, events were occurring in the library community that would make the creation of a national newspaper database a practical possibility. The development of the MARC formats by the Library of Congress, beginning in the late 1960s, and the establishment of the Online College Library Center's computer facility in the early 1970s offered a technical solution to the problems of setting up a national newspaper database. And the implementation of the CONSER (Conversion of Serials) Program in 1976 made possible the requirements of bibliographic standards, quality control and project coordination.

The CONSER Program was, and is, a cooperative effort to build a database of serials cataloging information through use of the OCLC Online Union Catalog. CONSER participants enter and upgrade cataloging records on OCLC according to standard guidelines, and these records are then authenticated by Centers of Responsibility, including the Library of Congress. Such records are available online from OCLC, and are distributed to others through the MARC Serials Distribution Service of the Library of Congress. Initially, only a limited number of institutions were authorized as CONSER participants, but the number has subsequently been expanded significantly.

The Library of Congress announced in 1974 that it would begin cataloging its newspaper collection, and in late 1975 announced that it would incorporate the records this produced into the CONSER database. It was recognized, however, that newspaper records had specialized requirements and that there was a need to analyze these requirements, to write specific cataloging instructions for newspapers, and to amend the CONSER guidelines accordingly. Because of the demand on staff time in implementing CONSER, LC was unable to cite a specific time when it could undertake these tasks.

Obviously, the needs of the historical community as evinced by the fledgling USNP and the solutions offered by the library community were destined to meet. The catalyst for this meeting was Larry G. Livingston of the Council on Library Resources, who was also a member of the USNP Advisory Panel. He perceived that the basic concepts of CONSER and the USNP were similar and that the problems to be solved were more those of timing and funding than of concept or design. To solve the immediate need to prepare a newspaper cataloging manual and to formulate CONSER guidelines for newspaper, Livingston located a consultant to work with LC in accomplishing this task. At the same time, OAH requested and received a grant from the Carnegie Foundation of New York to fund the work.

FIRST STEP—HOW TO CATALOG A NEWSPAPER

Work on the newspaper cataloging manual was begun in late 1977, a time when library cataloging rules were undergoing revision. The second edition of the *Anglo-American Cataloging Rules* was still in draft form, and implementation of the new rules was not expected until 1980. This imminent change in cataloging rules proved to be a blessing in disguise for the newspaper project. LC agreed to adopt an early recommendation that the newspaper manual be based on

AACR2. This would allow all newspapers entered into the CONSER database to be cataloged under the same rules, leading to a cleaner and more consistent database.*

In developing the newspaper manual, a serious attempt was made to fulfill the sometimes conflicting requirements of librarians, bibliographers and newspaper users. Problems arose in two major areas: (1) the definition of a newspaper; and (2) AACR2 rules for creating separate records.

No consistently applied definition of the term "newspaper" was available to the library community. The beginning of a decentralized national effort to enter newspaper entries into an online database, however, made a standard definition imperative. The definition agreed upon was developed by the Library of Congress, and is compatible with the definition adopted by the American National Information Standards Organization's Z39.39 Subcommittee. In drawing it up, one general assumption was held to: that the definition of a newspaper should be based primarily on content and readership, and not on the physical medium in which it is published. Briefly, the definition states that "a newspaper . . . contains news on all subjects . . . [and is] intended for the general public."[4] This definition includes most ethnic newspapers, but excludes newspapers intended in general for members of organizations or for a special clientele, those containing a special subject matter and those issued primarily for advertising purposes.

The requirements of newspapers dictated that the newspaper rules deviate from AACR2 in two major areas. The AACR2 requirement that separate records should be made if any of the first five words of the title changed was inappropriate for newspapers, where titles frequently fluctuate back and forth. It was recommended and accepted that separate records be made for title changes in newspapers only if the title variation appeared continuously for more than one year.

The most critical and necessary deviation from AACR2 for newspaper records was in the treatment of microforms and other reproductions. AACR2 specifies that separate records must be made when (a) an item has holdings in more than one physical medium, e.g., print, microfilm, photocopy, etc., *and* (b) when the producer of the reproduction changes and when the bibliographic description is based on the reproduction. Since newspaper holdings in most institutions are a

---

*__Editor's Note:__ Some pre-AACR2 newspaper records had been tape-loaded into the CONSER file from the Minnesota Union List of Serials, the Pittsburgh Union List of Serials and the Florida Union List of Serials; but within the realm of possible newspaper records, their number was minimal.

mix of newsprint, commercial microfilm, in-house microfilm and photocopies, etc. this rule was unacceptable. And since institutions with newspaper holdings may each have a different mix of print and reproductions, a union list of newspapers could conceivably have dozens of records for one title, even when only a few institutions held the title. Adding normal title changes in such a case and piecing all the records together would become complex, telling "who had what" in a union list next to impossible. In developing the newspaper cataloging rules, LC agreed to an interpretation for newspapers in which the physical form of the item was recorded in a holdings statement. In what has become known as the "master record convention," separate records are not made for different reproductions, but rather the bibliographic description of the newspaper is based on the original, i.e., newsprint, edition, and other physical forms are indicated in the holdings of the institution.

The cataloging manual was finished in draft form in late 1978, and in April, 1979, LC hosted a workshop on the new rules. Changes from this workshop and from continuing LC interpretation of AACR2 were later incorporated into the manual, and the first edition was published in 1981.

Meanwhile, the National Endowment for the Humanities had been taking an active role in formulating long-term plans for a national newspaper program. In 1978, the Endowment announced that it was prepared to commit itself to a ten- or fifteen-year program, which was a significant departure from its normal practice of funding only short-term projects. The Endowment also announced that it would develop guidelines on what it expected from a newspaper project as well as on the general framework in which the work of describing, locating, and preserving newspapers in each state should be approached.

In 1982 the Endowment issued its procedures and guidelines for U.S. Newspaper Program Projects and the U.S. Newspaper Program was formally established.[5] These guidelines proposed that identification, location and preservation of newspapers could be accomplished most effectively on a state by state basis in three phases. Phase I was to be a planning project in which each state would survey its newspaper repositories, assess the status of bibliographic control and preservation, and prepare a plan for implementing bibliographic control of its holdings. Each state was urged to designate one institution within the state to act as a coordinating agency for the program. Phase II was to comprise the bibliographical control component of the program. In this all newspaper repository sites were to be inventoried, all unique titles cataloged according to the *Newspaper Cataloging Manual*, and all bibliographic data were to be entered into the OCLC Online Union Catalog as CONSER records. All local holdings were to be entered into the USNP union list maintained in the OCLC Union Listing Component of the Serials Control Subsystem, and each state was expected to publish a union list of its newspapers upon completion of Phase II. Once statewide bibliographic control had been achieved, the Endowment would provide funds on a one-for-one matching basis to support preservation microfilming of important newspapers. This preservation effort was envisioned as Phase III.

The USNP is jointly managed by the Endowment and the Library of Congress. The Endowment is responsible for overall policy direction and grant management; LC handles overall technical management, issues guidelines for cataloging and CONSER participation and provides technical consultation and training for individual state projects. This cooperative arrangement was formalized by an official agreement in 1984. Organizations carrying out individual newspaper projects were designated as specialized CONSER participants; and authentication of newspaper records has been decentralized, with each project responsible for authenticating the descriptive portion of the record.

In 1982, the first bibliographic grants under the new guidelines were awarded to six large newspaper repositories: the American Antiquarian Society, the Center for Research Libraries, the Kansas State Historical Society, the New York Historical Society, the State Historical Society of Wisconsin, and the Western Reserve Historical Society. While still affirming that the statewide project was the most logical approach, the managers of the program believed that by converting these large collections, a core of records would be created to which, theoretically, individual states would need only add their holdings.*

In 1983, the first state-wide bibliographic grants were awarded to Montana and the Virgin Islands. Since that time, additional grants have been awarded each year until, at present, more than a dozen states are involved in Phase II bibliographic projects. A few have even completed that phase. Other states are involved in the planning phase. Individual state projects vary in their method of operation, yet all are exploring new territory in an attempt to unearth hidden collections of newspapers and establish new bonds of cooperation within the state.

As more states begin projects, the bibliographic phase will gain

---

*Editor's Note: In actual practice, a good deal of updating has had to be done to these records because the repositories tended to have scattered holdings of titles published outside of their geographic region, while the state projects had access to much fuller runs, often including earlier issues than those used by the repositories in their cataloging.

momentum. And as more newspapers titles are added to the CONSER database, progress should be faster, as it is expected that less original cataloging will be required. More importantly, as more institutional holdings are added, the preservation picture will become more clearly focused. Institutions with incomplete runs of titles will be able to locate issues to fill gaps and to pinpoint institutions with which cooperative arrangements would be beneficial. In 1986, NEH produced new guidelines that allow a state to combine bibliographic control and preservation phases of the program into one. This approach may reduce the time needed to complete the overall program by limiting the number of times a physical item need be handled.

WHAT REMAINS TO BE DONE?

The U.S. Newspaper Program is a massive undertaking and one of the most significant and beneficial information-related programs in many years. Yet despite the excellence of the program, there are still some matters that the library profession must address.

1. *Speed.* Various projections estimate that it will take twenty years for all of the fifty states to complete the USNP. The danger is that more newspapers will disintegrate before the program is completed. Is there a way to accelerate the work while still maintaining standards of high quality?

2. *Money.* Grants from the Endowment and matching non-federal funds may not suffice to allow a state to film every title published in the state, and states are urged to establish a selection criteria for preserving the more important research titles. Where else can money be found to preserve other needed titles?

3. *Specific holdings.* In order to allow institutions to locate copies of missing issues and to amalgamate scattered holdings into a complete set for preservation, specific holdings giving each issue held by an institution are necessary. The *USMARC Format for Holdings and Locations* (MFHL) was published in 1984, and the *American National Standard for Serial Holdings Statements* in mid-1986. These two publications define the standards for recording detailed holdings statements and for communicating them in machine-readable form. While neither OCLC nor the other bibliographic utilities have yet implemented the MFHL, should not the USNP management encourage the implementation of these standards?

4. *Enhanced cooperation.* The USNP has laid the foundation for excellent cooperation within the states. Should such coordinated efforts be extended to cooperative newspaper acquisition and collection

development programs? As institutions become aware of the holdings of others, agreements about which should be the "depository of record" for a particular title can be made, thus avoiding costly duplication. Is it desirable to establish collection and depository guidelines by which such agreements can be formalized?

5. *Non-extant titles.* The USNP guidelines discourages participants from reporting non-extant copies since one cannot describe what does not exist. Should a special minimal record be allowed that describes titles found only in reference works? Will issues of these titles be located some day?

6. *Indexing and desktop publishing.* Upon its completion, the USNP will have allowed us to locate, describe and preserve our newspapers. Should the next step be determining how to gain effective access to their contents? While indexes to more than thirty newspapers are available by way of commercial online information services, these are indexes to large daily newspapers and generally exclude regional and local news. Electronic desktop publishing, a topic of great current interest in the microcomputer world, may have an effect on newspapers. Given the relatively low cost of microcomputers and laser printers and the availability of page composition programs, many entrepreneurs may enter the newspaper publishing field. Yet the same technology that could increase the number of small newspapers, might also help unlock the contents of these papers. Word processing programs are available that will automatically, or semiautomatically, index a newspaper as it is typed. This feature could be a boon to the historian looking for a specific local event or the genealogist looking for names and dates. What role should the library profession play in this area?

Newspapers are as much a part of the American heritage as the Statue of Liberty. It is only fitting that librarians, as managers of this precious resource, observe the commitment embodied in the USNP by continuing to search for new ways to make newspapers and their contents more accessible to both the scholarly community and the general public.

NOTES

1. Gregory, Winifred, ed. *American Newspapers, 1821-1936; A Union List of Files Available in the United States and Canada.* (New York: H.W. Wilson, 1937.)
2. Brigham, Clarence S. *History and Bibliography of American Newspapers, 1690-1820.* (Westport, Conn.: Greenwood Press, 1976, c1975.)
3. *Newspapers in Microform: United States, 1948-1983.* (Washington: Library of Congress, 1972-1984.)

4. Harriman, Robert B. *Newspaper Cataloging Manual*. CONSER/USNP Ed. (Washington: Library of Congress, 1984.)

5. *Procedures and Standards for U.S. Newspaper Program Projects*. (Washington: National Endowment for the Humanities [1982].)

Creating a Newspaper Bibliography: The Indiana Newspaper Bibliography Project

John W. Miller

SUMMARY. The *Indiana Newspaper Bibliography* was the result of a special project of the Indiana Historical Society, carried out between 1978 and 1981. The *Bibliography* contains the following information for each newspaper published in Indiana between 1804 and 1980: (1) an historical narrative that includes the place of publication; all known titles; publication frequency; establishment, merger, and termination dates; political and special-interest affiliation; languages used if other than English; and all known editors and publishers, and (2) holdings information with data on original and microfilm copy locations. With the publication of the *Indiana Newspaper Bibliography*, researchers now have access to detailed information on each of Indiana's 8,000 newspaper titles. Thus loss of time and duplicated efforts throughout the state have been reduced.

In the spring of 1978 the Board of Trustees of the Indiana Historical Society approved the *Indiana Newspaper Bibliography* project, a three-year project designed to produce a bibliography of all Indiana newspapers published between 1804 and 1980, including locational data for all original and microfilm copies. The project began on fresh ground, in part because there were no national standards for newspaper bibliographies and in part because it was determined that Indiana's bibliography should include more material than had previous bibliographies in other states.

Following the hiring of the project director and two research assistants, planning for the implementation of the *Indiana Newspaper Bib-*

John W. Miller is the director of the Indiana Historical Society's Newspaper Microfilm Project, and was director of the Society's *Indiana Newspaper Bibliography* project. He holds a PhD degree in American History from Purdue University, and has written the *Indiana Newspaper Bibliography* and several articles on Indiana newspapers, the Black Hawk War, and technology in the workplace. Mailing address: Indiana Historical Society, 315 W. Ohio Street, Indianapolis, IN 46202.

liography began with the project director's attendance at a conference in Iowa City, Iowa, that was sponsored by the Organization of American Historians and the National Endowment for the Humanities. At this conference (which helped formulate guidelines for what has since become the United States Newspaper Project) discussions were held with newspaper research experts from throughout the country. Paul Stellhorn, Stephen Gutgesell, and Al Schroder (who had recently compiled guides to newspapers in New Jersey, Ohio, and Iowa) offered excellent advice on what to do and what to avoid in a newspaper bibliography project.

An immediate priority for the project was a definition of just what constituted a "newspaper." Several newspaper definitions were available, and the project wanted to use a definition that would be of the greatest value to potential users. Of some concern was whether to include special interest newspapers, such as ethnic, religious, labor, collegiate, temperance, and political campaign journals. In addition, there are occasions when it is difficult to decide whether a publication is a newspaper or not—does one consider appearance, philosophy, use, or some other criteria in evaluation? After consultation with several potential user groups, the *Indiana Newspaper Bibliography* definition of a newspaper was established as "a serial publication that has the appearance of a newspaper, considers itself a newspaper, is published at least twice a month, and includes general news and features or topical news of interest to a special interest group—such as ethnic, religious, collegiate, labor, farm, education, reform, military, and suburban." The project's definition of a newspaper was broader than the Library of Congress definition because it was determined that many researchers would be concerned with the special interest press.

A successful newspaper bibliography project requires full-time commitments from project staff; a project cannot rely on personnel who work on the project "when they have time." In the selection of project personnel, care was taken to envision project needs, to study the capabilities and flexibility of potential employees, and to hire compatible personalities. Competent clerical assistance was deemed crucial for the success of the project; someone had to keep track of the thousands of research notes, inventory sheets, questionnaire forms, correspondence, and other project records. It was correctly assumed that the best person to handle these duties was a competent secretary, and a detailed flow chart of procedures and sequences was used to keep track of the flow of records from person to person in the project.

Since the best sources of information on newspapers are the newspapers themselves, the *Indiana Newspaper Bibliography* project directly examined thousands of newspaper issues at the Indiana State Library and at over 200 repositories around the state. Available newspaper files provided direct verification of publication dates, title changes, editors and publishers, political affiliation, and special interests.

For newspaper titles with no extant copies, however, other sources had to be consulted. Perhaps the most reliable secondary sources were the national newspaper directories, published from the mid-nineteenth century to the present. The two most complete directories were G. P. Rowell's *American Newspaper Directory* (published yearly from 1869 to 1908) and N. W. Ayer's *Directory of Newspapers and Periodicals* (published yearly from 1880 to the present). These directories contained information on newspaper titles, editors and publishers, political affiliation, frequency of publication, and other useful data. One of the largest single research tasks of the *bibliography* project was the compilation of thousands of isolated bits of information from Rowell's and Ayer's directories and the arrangement of the data in an organized manner for each newspaper title. One thousand hours were spent obtaining this information and 3,000 information sheets were filled out with appropriate data. Unfortunately, since the newspaper directories went back only to 1870, about half of the newspaper titles published in Indiana were not included in the directories.

Three national bibliographies that list newspapers and their availability for each state were used: Clarence Brigham, *History and Bibliography of American Newspapers, 1690-1820*; Winifred Gregory, *American Newspapers, 1821-1936*; and *Newspapers in Microform: United States* (updated periodically). Gregory's volume (a WPA project undertaken during the Great Depression) has been the standard reference source for nearly fifty years for newspaper titles and location, but it does not include data on editors, publishers, political affiliation, or languages other than English. In addition, since the Gregory information has never been updated, none of the hundreds of thousands of newspaper microfilm reels that have been produced since the 1930s were included, and scores of original newspaper collections have since been moved from one repository to another or have been lost or destroyed. In addition to these sources, reference was had to a number of national newspaper bibliographies that contained information on special interest newspapers, such as black and German publications.

It was found that most histories of Indiana contained a brief section on the state's newspapers, and each of the ninety-two counties had at least one historical account of the area. These county histories contained information about the county's newspapers, but the many inaccuracies and omissions in these sources substantially limited their usefulness. Moreover, since most of Indiana's county histories were written in the late nineteenth century, information was available only for newspapers that had been published before that time. Several county atlases were consulted that contained brief descriptions of a county's newspaper heritage, and histories often written in conjunction with a centennial observance, were also used. Similarly, useful were centennial and souvenir editions of Indiana newspapers, as these usually include detailed accounts of the paper's journalistic history and occasionally featured the recollections of older newspapermen.

A number of theses and dissertations on Indiana newspapers were located, although the majority were limited to one newspaper or editor. Especially helpful were those few that dealt with the newspapers of an entire county, as was the author's doctoral dissertation on the pioneer press. A few manuscript collections were found that had detailed information on nineteenth century Indiana newspapers, and some state agencies held files of material on Indiana newspapers. In addition, a number of excellent articles on Indiana newspapers have been written in various journals over the years, especially on the subjects of the pioneer period and the special interest press.

In the introduction to the *Indiana Newspaper Bibliography*, potential users were alerted to the fact that the project staff realized the *Bibliography* contained several errors; but in cases where founding and termination dates, spelling of names and newspaper titles, and other information in the *Bibliography* differed from statements given in county histories and other secondary sources, this often implied that direct examination of newspapers or other reliable evidence had revealed information that conflicted with those sources. In fact, there were so many spelling and factual errors in most county histories that users of the *Bibliography* were warned to expect numerous discrepancies between the county histories and the *Bibliography*. Conflicts among sources are common, and as the *Bibliography* was compiled, reliance was placed, as time and availability permitted, on actual copies of the newspapers themselves.

In order to obtain newspaper information from Indiana repositories, questionnaires on newspaper history and availability were mailed early in the project to over 800 Indiana libraries, historical societies, museums, courthouses, and newspaper offices. In addition, requests for information were sent to several newspaper repositories in surrounding states and to the Library of Congress and the American Antiquarian Society. While most respondents were cooperative, some wrote back to say they did not have the time or inclination to answer the request for information, and a few did not return the questionnaire or respond to follow-up requests. The reasons for the occasional lack of cooperation seemed to include indifference, a fear that some state agency would try to take away their newspaper collection, and (especially among newspaper office personnel) a fear that researchers would ask to use newspaper collections that the owners wanted to keep undisturbed.

Some respondents misunderstood what was asked — they thought they were being asked to research holdings at all area repositories — although the instructions clearly indicated that only information about their repository was wanted. The most serious problem encountered was the high degree of incomplete and inaccurate information received from the repositories. It was discovered that many libraries, newspaper offices, historical societies, museums, and courthouses had little accurate information on their newspaper holdings. At many repositories, for example, what the staff believed to be complete runs of a newspaper title were later found to contain large gaps; at other locations, direct examination of the newspaper holdings turned up numerous volumes that had not been reported.

In light of the uneven responses to the questionnaires, it was decided that it would be necessary for project staff to visit as many of the repositories as possible to inventory collections and to obtain newspaper information. As a result, over 200 repositories in almost every county in Indiana were visited, and it became the recommendation of the *Indiana Newspaper Project* staff that future newspaper projects should plan to travel to repositories to the extent that money and time allow. If necessary, assistance should be obtained from volunteers and summer students, but comments from directors of previous projects indicate that uneven results can be expected when this is done. Ideally, a project should check every issue of every paper at all known repositories; but in most states this would cover millions of pages and consume years of staff time. The usual compromise of time and money, in past projects led in the present instance to detailed checking of papers at central repositories and a cursory scanning of titles at other locations, when possible.

Following consultation with several potential users of the *Indiana Newspaper Bibliography*, it was determined that (1) grouping minor title variations under the same main title entry and (2) ignoring articles ("a" and "the"), places of publication, and frequency of publication (daily, morning, weekly, etc.) for the purpose of newspaper alphabetization would be invaluable aids to researchers. These procedures were designed to facilitate the use of the *Bibliography* by researchers who knew only the general name of a newspaper, and not, for example, whether it was officially known as the *Clovertown Bee, Weekly Bee, Morning Bee,* or *Clovertown Daily Bee.* The *Bibliography* listed all these minor title variations under the main title *Bee,* with cross-references from all variant titles. Another reason for this usage was that many newspaper repositories have inventoried their newspapers by one major title only and have not maintained separate records for each minor title change.

Library of Congress symbols were obtained and used to eliminate the need to spell out the full name of a repository each time it was used. For example, the collection of microfilm copies of the *Lafayette American* at the American Antiquarian Society was listed as "MWA (M)" to indicate the location of the repository "MWA" and that the collection was on microfilm "(M)" instead of original "(O)." It was especially valuable for researchers to learn of the availability of microfilm copies at a repository, since the microfilm copies could be sent to any location in the country via interlibrary loan—an impossibility with original newspapers.

Since many newspaper collections were not complete, the designations "complete," "partial," and "scattered" were used in the locational data area to describe repository holdings. "Partial" indicated that the collection was less than 90% complete, and "scattered" meant six or fewer issues per year were available (exact dates were given in the locational data for scattered holdings). "Current only" holdings of repositories were not included in the *Bibliography*, since these holdings were removed from the repository after a brief time.

Several previous newspaper bibliography projects had wanted to collect information on editors and publishers, but had given up the effort. The primary reasons offered for stopping were the enormous amount of time needed to compile the information and the confusing nature of many newspaper ownership patterns, which included partial interests, family member involvements, and constant buying and selling by owners. The Indiana project succeeded in collecting such information because of both the determination of project staff to collect and utilize this data and the availability of certain information sources, including newspaper directories for the post-1870 period, manuscript notes on hundreds of nineteenth century newspapers, and "adequate" secondary sources.

Likewise, attempts by bibliography projects to identify the political affiliation of newspapers have had only limited success. In Iowa, for example, project personnel found the political party shifts by newspapers from Democrat to Republican to Independent and all shades in between too difficult to follow. Therefore, they noted only minor political parties and special interest newspapers. The Indiana project was able to obtain political affiliation labels for most newspapers, but the *Bibliography* warned potential users that some journals constantly switched political allegiance and that a number of nineteenth century newspapers claimed to support one party while they campaigned for another party's presidential candidate.

Several research aids were provided in the *Bibliography*, including a cross-reference index of Indiana towns and counties, an outline map of Indiana counties, and an index of 10,000 Indiana editors and publishers. The editor and publisher index (which is not available in most newspaper bibliographies) is useful when one tries to follow the travels of itinerant journalists who attempted newspaper ventures in the nineteenth century. These pioneers often established a newspaper operation in a new village, and then if prospects did not look good, they merely packed up their press and equipment and headed for the next town. Following the Civil War, however, newspaper operations became larger and more sophisticated, and journalists remained longer in one location.

In regard to the final format of the *Indiana Newspaper Bibliography*, it was decided to produce a hardbound book and to try to prepare a product that was neat, organized, and professional in appearance. The *Bibliography* staff was convinced it was of the utmost importance that information be conveyed effectively to the reader, as otherwise the whole point of the project would be lost. It was discovered that many printing companies had little experience with bibliography formats, and several were consulted before the contract was offered to a company with a history of producing products of good quality.

One of the more important expectations of the Indiana Historical Society *Newspaper Bibliography Project* was that publication of the *Bibliography* would encourage an increased interest in Indiana newspapers. This expectation has certainly been achieved; many previously unknown newspaper titles have been discovered in attics, storage rooms, and other locations. The *Bibliography* has also had a positive effect on newspaper preservation in Indiana. One effort in this direction was the creation of the Indiana Historical Society Newspaper Microfilm Project, which has microfilmed over three million pages of Indiana newspapers since 1980.

In conclusion, it can be observed that before publication of the *Indiana Newspaper Bibliography*, researchers had little way of knowing which newspaper collections were available in the state. Researchers in Fort Wayne seeking information on Evansville newspapers could call or write all the repositories in Vanderburgh County, but this was time-consuming and/or costly. They were also faced with checking at the Indiana State Library, Indiana University, and other repositories throughout the state for additional possible locations. If the researcher was looking for data on editors and publishers, it was also necessary to consult county histories, manuscript sources, biographical directories, and other materials.

The *Indiana Newspaper Bibliography* provides the answers to the above and other research questions about Indiana newspapers. It now takes only a few minutes to find out if there was a Populist journal published at Logansport in the 1890s or to prepare a list of all Whig papers printed in Indianapolis in the first half of the nineteenth century. Researchers no longer have to travel around the state to see if a particular paper was a reform journal, a political organ, or a literary sheet, and they know immediately which years of the paper are available for examination at any of the state's hundreds of newspaper repositories.

Uniform Titles for Newspapers: A Proposal

Lois N. Upham

SUMMARY. Following a discussion of some basic problems associated with the cataloging of newspapers, this article discusses the main protocols used by the U.S. Newspaper Project in dealing with title variations. A general discussion of the concept of uniform titles as they are currently applied to newspapers is then presented, and this is followed by a proposal to revert to the "traditional" concept of uniform titles. It is argued that this change would be beneficial to both the creators and the users of newspaper bibliographies. A possible format is suggested.

THE PROBLEM

Bibliographic control of newspapers has always been a difficult task, at best. The volatile nature of nearly every aspect of the format—frequency, size, publisher, place of publication, and, most importantly, title—makes the creation of a reliable bibliographic record a risky venture.

The way that most patrons access newspaper files is through use of a combination of geographic location, title and date. Of these three the title usually presents greatest difficulty for both patron and curator. This difficulty can be the result of one or several closely related problems. The most obvious problem is the fact that newspaper titles, especially in the last century, tended to change often. A closely related problem is the existence at different times or at the same time of several newspapers with the same title. These duplicate titles can be held by totally distinct papers from the same or different geographic locations or can result from the reassumption of an earlier title by the same paper.

Lois Upham holds a BA from the University of Maryland, the MSLS degree from UNC-Chapel Hill, and the PhD from North Texas State University. She is an assistant professor in the College of Library and Information Science at the University of South Carolina, Columbia where she teaches courses in the areas of Technical Services and Automation.

In the early history of the United States, ownership of newspapers changed hands often. Sometimes partnerships were formed; sometimes partners bought out one another's interests. Changes in political affiliation often occurred, and publishers even picked up their presses and moved to new locations in the hope of procuring a larger readership and more paying subscribers. Each of these occurrences presented a tempting opportunity for a change in title. Whereas today the temptation might be resisted, in past times it was more often than not happily seized upon. Some of the more fascinating occurrences of title changing came about when the members of what had originally been a partnership repeatedly bought out each other's interests. The result could be both amusing and — especially to a cataloger — frustrating. Each it seemed would *have* to change the title with every new appropriation, as if doing so somehow established their basic territorial rights. The result, if not confusing to readers of the day (one suspects there was confusion), is certainly cause for bafflement among today's patrons. An added difficulty occurred with the advent of varying editions, especially ones of differing frequency, which then required title adjustments to allow patrons to discriminate among them. The following is an actual sequence of titles that illustrates a typical set of variations:

    NATIONAL VOLUNTEER
    SHELBY VOLUNTEER
    NATIONAL VOLUNTEER
    SHELBY NATIONAL VOLUNTEER
    SHELBYVILLE VOLUNTEER
    SHELBYVILLE WEEKLY VOLUNTEER
    SHELBYVILLE VOLUNTEER
    SHELBYVILLE WEEKLY VOLUNTEER
    SHELBY DEMOCRAT-VOLUNTEER
    SHELBY DEMOCRAT
    SHELBYVILLE DEMOCRAT (daily)
    SHELBYVILLE DEMOCRAT (weekly)

NOTE: Shelby is a county; Shelbyville is a city within that county.

As has been stated in Woods' article found elsewhere in this volume, as well as in the Summer 1986 issue of *Cataloging & Classification Quarterly*, the U.S. Newspaper Project has established protocols for cataloging newspapers. Two important ones address problems associated with the cataloging of fluctuating titles and with the handling of duplicate titles. These are:

Variations in title. If a newspaper title fluctuates back and forth over a period of time, and the variant title appears continuously for no more than a year at a time, separate records are not justified. Choose the title of the first issue (or earliest issue in hand) as the title proper. Record the variant title as an access point and in a note. Record inclusive dates and/or issue numbers if available. If, however, a newspaper is published under the variant title for more than one year at a time, separate records for each title are required.

Uniform title headings. Create a uniform title heading for a newspaper if the title proper of the newspaper is identical to the title proper of another serial in the catalog, regardless of whether the other serial is entered under title or under a name heading. (The catalog referred to here is the file or files against which the searching and cataloging is being done.) Take into account only the title proper of another serial, not variants traced as cross references or as added entries.[1]

Although these instructions at first seem to address different problems, they are, in fact, closely related and can be cause for confusion if it is necessary to apply them both to the same sequence of titles. If, for instance, in the sequence of newspaper titles given above, the first *National Volunteer* had lasted less than a year, the cataloger might, according to the instructions in **Variations in title** skip to the second title and merely acknowledge the existence of the first title by giving it an added access point and a note. This decision would not, however, be consistent with the directive to "choose the title of the first issue," and it would also be contrary to AACR2. In Chapter 12 of AACR2 it is stated that information about the title and statement of responsibility should come from the chief source of information, and that the chief source should be from . . . "the first issue of the serial, [or] failing this, . . . [from] the first issue that is available."[2] Further, consider the possibility that the first *Shelbyville Weekly Volunteer* lasted for several years, but that the second one was only published for a few months. According to the first directive given above, the title that only lasted for only a few months should not be cataloged separately, but the first should be. According to the second directive, the paper that duplicated the first title should be given a uniform title, and depending upon what may be discovered in the catalog, the first *Shelbyville Volunteer* may or may not require one—unless, of course issues of that title are not discovered until after issues of the "second" title have already been handled.

Still, the basic incompatibility of these instructions may not be completely evident until it is remembered that the 246 (Varying Form of Title) field does not accommodate a uniform title. Yet a 246 field is where the existence of the short-lived *Shelbyville Volunteer* would be recorded and upon which the added access point would be based. Thus, if the titles are not cataloged separately, confusion would result from the fact that duplicate titles within a single sequence were not uniquely identified. Even if the titles were parts of separate title groups, it might not be possible to distinguish easily among them without some time-consuming research.

UNIFORM TITLES

Before proceeding further with this discussion it is appropriate to discuss the concept of the "uniform titles." In recent times the definition of this term has undergone revision. In the original edition of AACR2 the definition was as follows:

> **Uniform title.** 1. The particular title by which a work that has appeared under varying titles is to be identified for cataloguing purposes. 2. A conventional collective title used to collocate publications of an author, composer, or corporate body containing several works or extracts, etc., from several works, e.g., complete works, several works in a particular literary or musical form.[3]

The first set of rule revisions, however, provided a new definition for the term. It replaced definition "1," added a completely new "2," and renumbered "2" above as "3." The new and replaced sections read as follows:

> **Uniform title.** 1. The particular title by which a work is to be identified for cataloging purposes. 2. The particular title used to distinguish the heading for a work from the heading for a different work. 3. [The same as 2. in the original AACR2 definition].[4]

Number two is the definition used in the *Newspaper Cataloging Manual*. The very use of the term "uniform" seems, however, to be misleading when it is considered that the purpose of the entity which purports to be uniform is to distinguish uniquely. In *Webster's New Collegiate Dictionary* the following definition of the word "uniform" is given:

Uniform. 1. having always the same form, manner, or degree: not varying or variable; 2. of the same form with others: conforming to one rule or mode; 3. presenting an undiversified appearance of surface, pattern, or color; 4. consistent in conduct or opinion.[5]

Given this definition, the use of the term "uniform title" to identify an entity the purpose of which is the exact opposite of uniformity certainly seems contradictory at best.

The Proposal

John Miller in his article "Creating a Newspaper Bibliography," which is found elsewhere in this volume, states that

> following consultation with several users of the *Indiana Newspaper Bibliography*, it was determined the 1) grouping minor title variations under the same main title entry and 2) ignoring articles . . . , places of publication, and frequency of publication . . . for the purpose of newspaper alphabetization would be invaluable aids to researchers. These procedures were designed to facilitate the use of the *Bibliography* by researchers who knew only the general name of a newspaper, and not, for example, whether it was officially known as the *Cloverton bee, Weekly bee, Morning bee*, or *Cloverton daily bee*. The *Bibliography* listed all these minor title variations under the main title *Bee* . . .

This decision is actually more in keeping with the original uniform title concept than is the practice followed in the U.S. Newspaper Project. It is not in and of itself, however, a sufficient substitute for current USNP practices. For instance, in the Miller bibliography, even significantly varying titles are not given added access points, and information (especially about dates and geographical location) crucial to unique identification is not included.

Given the wild variations in newspaper titles—both in terms of number and repetition—a return to the original concept of the uniform title would seem logical for this format. A newspaper uniform title could truly be a "particular title by which a work that has appeared under varying titles is to be identified for cataloguing purposes."[6] The concept stated by Miller of choosing the consistently recurring keyword or words would seem to be logical. In the sequence of Shelby County titles given previously, the keyword would be "Volunteer," until the change to "Democrat-Volunteer occurred." Thus, there would be one entry in the catalog for the "Volunteer" sequence rather than the up to eight entries that would need to be used now. Since "Volunteer" would obviously be insufficient to pull together only the papers from Shelbyville, Shelby County, qualifiers would have to be added. The most obvious of these would be geographic location, following the rules outlined in Chapter 23 of AACR2. Inclusive dates of this record could then be added. Since there are no "perfect solutions," it is recognized that there would still be a problem with editions of differing frequency that were being published within the same sequence simultaneously and that contained the same basic keywords in their titles. Even, however, if it were necessary to enter separate records to reflect each frequency, there would still be a substantial reduction in the total number of records created.

The Proposed Record

Using the sequence of "Volunteer" titles from Shelby County which is given above, the following is a proposal of how the title related fields of a record that employs a **true** uniform title might look:

```
. . .
130 00 VOLUNTEER (Shelbyville, Ind. : 1844-1880)
245 14 NATIONAL VOLUNTEER
246 10 SHELBY VOLUNTEER
246 10 SHELBYVILLE VOLUNTEER
246 10 SHELBYVILLE WEEKLY VOLUNTEER

. . .
500     From [date-date] called: NATIONAL VOLUNTEER;
        from [date-date] called: SHELBY VOLUNTEER; from
        [date-date] called: NATIONAL VOLUNTEER; from
        [date-date] called: SHELBY NATIONAL VOLUN-
        TEER; from [date-date] called: SHELBYVILLE VOL-
        UNTEER; from [date-date] called: SHELBYVILLE
        WEEKLY VOLUNTEER; from [date-date] called:
        SHELBYVILLE VOLUNTEER; from [date-date]
        called: SHELBYVILLE WEEKLY VOLUNTEER.

. . .
785 07 SHELBY DEMOCRAT
785 07 SHELBY DEMOCRAT-VOLUNTEER
. . .
```

Obviously, other variations could appear in such a format. As shown above, the 245 (Title statement) field contains the earliest title in this sequence. This is in keeping with AACR2 instructions to catalog from the earliest piece. The 246 (Varying form of title) fields could actually include the date span during which each title was effective, but adopting this approach would mean that multiple occurrences of the same title would either have to be given multiple 246 fields, or multiple date spans would have to be included in the ≠f. Further, as the notes that could be automatically generated from such 246 fields would likely be quite confusing, it might still be necessary for the cataloger to construct an explanatory note.

Despite the fact that there are undoubted improvements that can be made to this proposal, it is nevertheless submitted for consideration. It can be hoped that through discussion and evaluation a proposal containing a minimum number of problems can actually be formulated and adopted. The situation as it exists at present is becoming more and more untenable. If some changes are not made soon, by the time that all state and territorial projects are completed, there will be such a proliferation of duplicate (qualified and unqualified) titles in the database, and such an unevenness in the treatment of short-lived titles, that only the fortunate (and one assumes tenacious) patron will actually be able to locate a desired title in the resulting union list.

NOTES

1. Robert Harriman, *Newspaper Cataloging Manual: CONSER/USNP Edition* (Washington, D.C., 1984), pp. 32-34.
2. *Anglo-American Cataloguing Rules: Second Edition* (Chicago, Illinois, 1978), p. 249.
3. *Ibid.*, p. 572.
4. *Anglo-American Cataloguing Rules: Second Edition: Revisions* (Chicago, Illinois, 1982), inserted on p. 572 of the code proper.
5. *Webster's New Collegiate Dictionary* (Springfield, Mass., 1979), p. 1269.
6. *Anglo-American Cataloguing Rules: Second Edition, op. cit.*, p. 572.

The Physical Aspects of Newspaper Collection Management: Some Problems and Their Solution

Thomas D. Lund

SUMMARY. America's heritage as depicted in newspapers is threatened by a number of problems, among them deterioration of original newspapers and microfilm and a general lack of training in preservation techniques. How common such problems are is demonstrated by a sampling of some of America's archival repositories, state libraries, and historical society libraries. Suggestions are made concerning maintenance and preservation of newspaper collections.

In 1910, Frank P. Hill of the Brooklyn Public Library gave a speech on the problem of newsprint deterioration before the American Library Association. This was, of course, long before the development of micrographics technology which has come to be regarded as the means of solving the newsprint deterioration problem. Hill focused on the only recourse then available to libraries for coping with rapidly deteriorating newspaper collections: having preservation copies printed on high quality paper stock, coating existing collections with a "cellit" solution, and storing them properly in dark, cool locations.[1]

Hill's comments were duly noted and accepted at the ALA convention, but not put into practice. Newspaper publishers rejected his ideas regarding the printing of preservation copies because of the cost involved and the basic incompatibility of the recommended paper with their printing presses. Librarians also rejected his ideas on the proper storage of newspapers because the implementation of these ideas would have required more time and money than they were willing to spend on newspapers. As a result, many pre-1910 newspapers that

---

Thomas D. Lund was a staff member of the Indiana Newspaper Project located at the Indiana State Library, 140 N. Senate Avenue, Indianapolis, IN 46204. He is currently a Senior Archives Assistant and is finishing his bachelor's degree at Indiana University-Purdue University, Indianapolis, majoring in Political Science and Geography.

would give researchers added insight into a rather turbulent period of our social history have probably long since crumbled into dust.

Today, seventy-six years later, not much has changed in the area of newspaper preservation, and in many respects the problem that most concerned Hill — preservation of newspapers as a source of local history — is still with us today.

An important improvement in newspaper preservation, introduced in the late 1930s, was commercial microfilming. Microfilming has helped greatly to allow libraries to withdraw brittle issues from patron use and to reduce the bulk of their newspaper collections, while actually increasing patron utilization. This result, moreover, has been achieved at reasonable cost.

Microfilming has come to be regarded as the most practical preservation technique now available. Hundreds of commercial and institutional microfilming organizations are engaged in their microfilming of newspapers nationally, and acceptance of their products is universal. Newspaper deterioration, always an accepted fact, no longer is deemed the impediment to the use of newspapers that it was in the past. Microfilming has removed to a large degree the reliance by researchers and others on brittle newspapers.

Apart from newsprint deterioration, three major problems threaten the permanence of newspaper collections. One is that many librarians and archivists are not properly trained in the preservation of newspaper collections. Emphasis on theory rather than application in some library schools leaves newspaper library staffs ill equipped to deal with the preservation of their collections.[2] If training in the maintenance and preservation of newspaper collections is lacking, it is not surprising that mistakes are made. Most such training is in fact acquired on the job. There are marked differences between an ordinary library collection and a newspaper collection, and these differences deserve emphasis in library school curriculums.

Newspapers lack certain of the characteristics of other library materials. Newspapers, moreover, are not in general amenable to control by the various identification systems used in libraries. Another characteristic that distinguishes newspapers from other library materials is their size. This factor alone usually necessitates the storage of newspapers away from other library materials, as indeed does the bulk of volumes accumulated over time.

The second problem concerns the sporadic use of quality control methods by some microfilming companies. A positive reel of poor quality is a problem that can go undetected until the reels are requested and viewed. When a problem with positive copy is identified, it is often too late for effective action to be taken. As the original newspapers have long since been discarded, refilming is not possible. There is always the original negative reel to rely on, of course, if it is within access, unless the problem was in the original microfilming. Lack of quality control is a serious concern, for when reels of poor quality cannot be replaced with corrected reels, the original newspapers must be retained. Bad reels, in fact, may never be replaced because the newspapers may have deteriorated beyond the point at which remicrofilming them is possible.

The third problem concerns the fact that microfilm, like newsprint, can be adversely affected by the environment in which it is stored. Estimates as to how long it takes for deterioration to occur vary. While it was previously thought that the shelf life of microfilm was fifty to 100 years, recent evidence indicates that it may be far shorter, depending upon the storage method used.[3] The chemical deterioration of microfilm is a slow process and the impact on the content of the microfilm may not appear until the deterioration is quite advanced. Since no test exists as yet to determine the effective shelf life of microfilm, definitive data in this area is lacking.

In an effort to ascertain whether the various problems encountered by the Indiana State Library Newspaper Section were typical of those in other repositories, a survey questionnaire (see Appendix 1) was mailed to sixteen archival repositories, state libraries, and state historical society libraries. These sixteen institutions were chosen through a random sampling of institutions in the fifty states. Of the sixteen, thirteen, or 81% responded.

The respondents were asked about their newspaper collections and the environment in which they are stored, in the case of both microfilmed newspapers and originals. They were also asked whether or not any restorative measures were currently underway (e.g., deacidification or cleaning and mending).

Regarding the overall physical condition of original newspapers in their collections, the respondents were allowed a scale of response ranging from very good to very poor. Six respondents (46.1%) indicated that their originals were in good condition. The remainder indicated that their collections fell into the fair (four respondents, 30.8%) and poor (three respondents, 23.1%) categories. None of the respondents answered "very good" or "very poor." Since the respondents were not asked to list what physical types of newspapers (i.e., cotton rag or woodpulp) were contained in their collections, the percentage of cotton rag newspapers versus those made out of woodpulp is not known. However, it is known that newspapers published before 1870 are probably of cotton rag, those published during the period 1870-1880 of mixed cotton rag/woodpulp composition, and those published after 1880 of woodpulp.[4]

The questionnaire included a list of time periods to aid in identifying the age of newspapers held in a particular collection. Six of the thirteen respondents had newspapers for every category listed from pre-1800 to the present. Three respondents had newspapers in five of the six categories, from the years 1801 to the present. Two of the respondents had newspapers from 1851 to the present in four of the six categories. The remaining two respondents had newspapers only from 1850 through 1925. The majority of the newspapers in the last group then would be of a cotton rag/woodpulp mixture or of woodpulp alone. Since such types of paper deteriorate fairly quickly, one would expect the investigated collections to be rated "poor." The two respondents in fact answered that their collections were in one case "fair" and in the other "poor."

Some of the respondents indicated that considerable work had been done to deacidify, clean, and encapsulate certain portions of their collections. They indicated further that newspapers made of woodpulp were in very bad condition and desperately needed to be microfilmed and the originals withdrawn from use. Newspapers published as recently as the early 1950s were found to be discolored and brittle; woodpulp newspapers that precede them were in worse condition; those published during the period 1890 through 1910 were virtually unusable.

Regarding the storage conditions of newspaper holdings, two separate questions were asked. The first requested information on how and where original newspapers were stored; the second on how and where newspaper microfilm is stored.

In evaluating the storage conditions used for original newspapers, respondents were asked to consider the temperature and humidity conditions of storage areas. The responses were: very good, one respondent (7.69%); good, four respondents (30.77%); fair, five respondents (38.46%); poor, one respondent (7.69%); and very poor, two respondents (15.39%). Those who elaborated on their responses admitted that while temperature and humidity were monitored, both tended to vary more than was desirable. The responses regarding the storing of newspaper copies indicated that newspapers were either bound in volumes or wrapped in brown craft paper. Standard metal library shelving was in general use.

The respondents were asked to rate the physical condition of their microfilm holdings. Six respondents (46.15%) answered that their microfilm was in very good condition, and another six (46.15%) answered good. One respondent (7.69%) failed to answer this question. The fact that there were no responses in the fair, poor and very poor categories attests to the storage advantages that microfilm has over original newspapers.

The respondents were consistent in their responses regarding the storage of microfilm. The microfilm is stored in multi-drawered metal microfilm cabinets. Several respondents indicated that in regard to their overall collection, the earliest newspapers had been microfilmed and that microfilming of the balance of their newspapers was either ongoing or in the planning stages. In most newspaper repositories, as stated earlier, preservation consists solely of microfilming. This effort is severely compromised, however, by those bent on saving the older, more ornate and oversized rag newspapers and not apparently concerning themselves with the woodpulp newspapers in their collections. The older cotton rag newspapers are in relatively good condition, even if they have been subjected to poor handling techniques and poor environmental conditions, while the newer woodpulp newspapers are crumbling into dust. The preoccupation with saving rag newspapers, which has, it is assumed, to do with their age, has the effect of using up funds in this effort that would be better applied to the immediate microfilming of newspaper holdings for the period 1890 through 1930. In many cases the woodpulp newspapers will be unrecognizable as holdings long before sufficient funds are allocated for their microfilming. In the current tight fiscal environment, it is sad to think that funding for microfilming might not be available in any case.

While some respondents indicated what restorative efforts besides microfilming were being undertaken to save their collections, none gave any information that indicated whether or not efforts were being made to evaluate the physical condition of their microfilm. Lack of microfilming quality control can lead to a particularly insidious problem, because poorly made microfilm can go undetected for long periods, if it is not used. In such cases, if, for whatever reason, the hard copy originals no longer exist, one can suppose that valuable material has been lost, perhaps forever. The problem can and often is further complicated by the fact that most larger repositories receive commercial microfilm from more than one source, not to mention microfilm that is produced in-house. The result is that microfilm of various levels of quality is constantly being added to collections. Some reels lack targets, which are labels used by the microfilmer to indicate such things as: the beginning and ending of the reel; resolution, reduction, and contrast charts; inventories of titles and dates microfilmed on a given reel; and month and year separations. Reels without targets are more difficult to interpret than properly targeted ones. Such reels then can be added to others that are badly scratched and mutilated from long years of use, that are shot out of focus or with black and white contrast that is so poor it is difficult to tell exactly what was filmed, or that have targets obscuring portions of pages. These flaws often go undetected until complaints are received about them, as often enough there is insufficient staff to allow for the checking of the microfilm for such flaws.

Since the root of the problem is that newspapers deteriorate and that newspaper microfilm does also, an effective method of preserving their narrative content must be sought. Given the technologies currently available or projected to be available in the near future, the laser disc seems to offer the permanence and indestructibility that are needed. As the contents of existing microfilm reels can be transferred easily onto laser discs, it seems only logical that laser discs be used in this way. The cost of this at the moment is high, but will surely drop, as is so with most new technological advances, when there is a sufficient market (witness the situation with compact discs, calculators, and computers).

In the meantime, efforts should be made to complete the microfilming of any and all newspapers of the period 1890-1930 that have not yet received this attention. It cannot be stressed enough that newspapers of this period are in generally horrible condition and every delay in their microfilming makes it more likely that they will be lost as a source of information. Moreover, costs associated with microfilming increase as newspapers deteriorate, for microfilming badly damaged items is an extremely difficult, time-consuming, and therefore costly process.

Microfilm collections should be inventoried, with identification of multiple-title microfilm reels given priority in the matter. This will help prevent unwanted duplication of holdings for a given title. Spot checking of reels for physical and narrative defects and reel carton labeling errors also needs to be undertaken.

Finally, and most importantly, library schools should include course work on newspapers and newspaper collection management in their curriculums. Whether or not the historical data contained in newspapers survives for posterity will depend heavily upon the efforts of librarians and archivists charged with their preservation. Graduates of library schools who work in newspaper libraries often come to their work without any relevant academic training, and are forced to learn everything on the job. While some may argue that this is all to the good, much time will inevitably be needed before what needs to be known is assimilated and put into practice. An academic foundation, particularly in the preservation of library materials, would be extremely helpful to all practitioners.

Whether or not progress made to this point in newspaper preservation continues depends upon various changes in current practice. And whether or not the changes occur depends upon how seriously librarians and archivists view the need for them.

NOTES

1. Hill, Frank P., The Deterioration of Newspaper, *Bulletin of the American Library Association*, Vol. IV, January-November, 1910, pp. 675-678.
2. Bansa, Helmut, The Awareness of Conservation. Reasons for Reorientation in Library Training, *Restaurator, The International Journal for the Preservation of Library and Archival Materials*, Vol. 7, No. 1, 1986, pp. 38-44.
3. Adelstein, P.Z., Preservation of Microfilm, *Journal of Micrographics*, Vol. 11, No. 6, July-August 1978, p. 336.
4. Cunha, George M. and Dorothy G., *Conservation of Library Materials. A Manual and Bibliography on the Care, Repair and Restoration of Library Materials*, Vol. I, The Scarecrow Press, Inc., Metuchen, N.J., 1971, 2nd Edition, pp. 121-122.

APPENDIX 1

NEWSPAPER HOLDINGS CONDITION QUESTIONNAIRE

Feel free to expand on any of your responses; use the reverse side of this sheet if you need extra space.

1. Do you have newspapers in your collection?   Yes   No

2. If your answer is yes, what is the relative age of your collection? (Circle ALL that apply.)

| pre-1800 to 1800 | 1801 to 1850 | 1851 to 1900 | 1901 to 1925 | 1926 to 1950 | 1951 to present |

3. In what format(s) are your newspapers held?

   Hard copy original   Microform   Both

4. If you have hard copy originals, describe basically where and how they are stored (e.g., on flat metal shelves in the main stack area, unbound and wrapped in brown paper bundles).

5. Rate the overall physical condition of your hard copy collection.

   Very good   Good   Fair   Poor   Very poor

APPENDIX 1 (continued)

6. Rate the physical conditions in which your hard copy holdings are stored. (NOTE: Take into account such things as proper temperature, humidity control, lighting, etc.)

    Very good   Good   Fair   Poor   Very poor

7. If you have newspapers on microform, describe basically how and where they are stored (e.g., in multidrawered metal microfilm cabinets in a special microfilm storage room).

8. Rate the physical condition of your microform holdings.

    Very good   Good   Fair   Poor   Very poor

9. Are any preservation efforts being made with regard to your newspaper collection?

    Yes   No

10. If yes, what is the nature of the effort (e.g., deacidification; cleaning/mending; filming—list what years or types of papers, if applicable; chemical evaluation of microfilm; etc.)?

The Microfilming of Newspapers — The Indiana Historical Society Newspaper Microfilm Project

John W. Miller

SUMMARY. The Indiana Historical Society Newspaper Microfilm Project has microfilmed over three million pages of Indiana newspapers in danger of deterioration or destruction. As newspapers are microfilmed, four major objectives are kept in mind—preservation, storage space savings, microfilm copy availability, and publicity. The microfilm process involves several procedures and negotiations with numerous agencies and individuals. One of the most important aspects of the project is the researching of newspaper collections in Indiana repositories, and there are several considerations for researchers to keep in mind as they work in these repositories.

The Indiana Historical Society Newspaper Microfilm Project began in the summer of 1980 with the goal of microfilming Indiana newspapers in danger of deterioration or destruction. The project has continued to the present time, and over three million pages of Indiana newspapers have been microfilmed. Before it ends in 1990, the project anticipates being able to microfilm all pre-1920 Indiana newspapers and a few additional collections from later years.

Before the Newspaper Microfilm Project could begin in 1980, problems of space, equipment, and personnel had to be solved. A home for the project was carved out of space in the basement of the Indiana State Library building, but not before significant remodeling, painting, and cleaning had taken place. Two 35mm planetary cameras were obtained, and additional equipment was purchased or borrowed from

---

John W. Miller is the director of the Indiana Historical Society's Newspaper Microfilm Project and was director of the Society's *Indiana Newspaper Bibliography* project. He holds a PhD degree in American History from Purdue University, and has written the *Indiana Newspaper Bibliography* and several articles on Indiana newspapers, the Black Hawk War, and technology in the workplace. Mailing address: Indiana Historical Society, 315 W. Ohio Street, Indianapolis, IN 46202.

other areas of the State Library building. Several experienced microfilmers were interviewed, and three were hired to work on the project.

As newspapers are microfilmed, four major objectives are kept in mind:

Preservation — Newspapers printed since the 1880s are made from woodpulp paper, which soon becomes brittle and eventually disintegrates. The Society's Newspaper Microfilm Project has replaced over three million pages of these deteriorating newspapers with microfilm copies. The microfilm is expected to last for several decades, and new copies can be made as the older microfilm begins to deteriorate.

Space — The Indiana State Library currently uses over 50,000 cubic feet of space to store its original newspaper collection. This space requirement will be reduced to less than 2,000 cubic feet when the entire collection is placed on microfilm, and similar savings on a smaller scale can be realized at libraries, historical societies and museums, courthouses, and newspaper offices around the state.

Availability — As original newspaper collections are filmed, microfilm copies become available at several locations. Access is not limited to the place where the originals are housed, as microfilm copies can be sent across the state or nation via interlibrary loan. Patron use at libraries and other repositories is made easier through the availability of microfilm copies, which are easier to service and store than original volumes.

Publicity — As the Newspaper Microfilm Project assists local historical agencies with planning for microfilming, evaluation of newspaper holdings, and conservation, closer ties are established between these agencies and the Indiana Historical Society. As the microfilm staff works throughout the state, the Society, in effect, gains additional field agents, who work with local agencies in areas of mutual concern.

Once the Newspaper Microfilm Project receives a stack of newspapers from a project participant, the papers are placed on storage shelves and assigned batch numbers. When the papers are scheduled for filming, they are moved to the filming room and a special cradle is used to remove any bindings. A detailed inventory of each newspaper batch is made, and torn or wrinkled pages are repaired with tape or smoothed with an electric iron. Then the newspapers are collated and arranged in chronological sequence by title, and film targets and inventory sheets are prepared for filming. The targets include the following sheets placed at the beginning of each reel: "start," a sheet of white paper used for a density check during processing, a resolution chart to test for film clarity, a sheet that gives the reduction ratio used during the filming process, a title sheet that lists the exact title and starting and ending dates of the issues included on the reel, a sheet that indicates the microfilm reel is not to be duplicated without the permission of the Indiana Historical Society, a sheet that shows the year the microfilm reel was made, and a sheet that indicates the best available copies were used for the filming. Month and year targets are also included throughout the reel as finding aids.

The newspapers are filmed one page at a time, and the film is removed from the cameras and assigned a reel number. The newspapers are then placed on holding shelves, and the negative film is taken to the processing room after a worksheet has been prepared that will follow the film through the remaining stages of production. After the negative film has been run through the processing machine, the film is inspected, checked for clarity and density, and spliced, when necessary. Labels are attached to the negative boxes. Using a positive print duplicator, positive print microfilm is prepared for sale to participants and for use at the State Library building by researchers and for interlibrary loan. Finally, the negative reels are placed in a protected vault and the original newspapers returned to their owners.

The filming of the Jeffersonville *Evening News* was typical of the filming of the hundreds of titles dealt with in the Society's project. The general manager of the *Evening News* considered the microfilming of his paper to be very valuable for the Jeffersonville community, since this paper opened up one of the best records of the history of Clark County. He remarked that the Society's newspaper microfilming project was "one of the greatest services to the community that the Indiana Historical Society could provide." Likewise, the director of the Jeffersonville Public Library noted that the preservation microfilming of the *Evening News* had been a goal of their library for some time and had been the special project of one of the reference librarians, who had worked to obtain some of the issues of the paper from the estate of a former publisher. The library had wanted to get the paper filmed for some years, but had been unable to get permission from the former owner, who kept the papers in a room with tremendous ranges of temperature and humidity. The papers were deteriorating rapidly, and the library's board of directors felt that something had to be done soon; they were elated when arrangements were finally made with the estate to allow for the filming. They considered the small cost of the filming to be a fine investment.

The advanced deterioration of the *Evening News* necessitated special handling and preparation procedures. Typical of woodpulp newspapers printed since the 1880s, many issues of the *Evening News* were in scraps when received by the Newspaper Microfilm Project. Nevertheless, armed with steam irons, rolls of tape, and a world of patience, the project staff was able to convert the papers to microfilm copies that can be used for years to come without worry about further deterioration.

When interested individuals contact the project about the possibility of having their newspaper collections microfilmed, they are asked to first contact local libraries, historical societies and museums, courthouses, newspaper offices, and interested individuals to determine if anyone has additional copies of the newspapers and to enlist the cooperation and assistance of others who may want their newspapers filmed. The next step for participants is to sort their collections into stacks by title and to arrange the papers in chronological order. The collections are then checked for major gaps, which are noted for reference. When these steps have been finished, the participants call the project office to set up a specific time for filming the collection.

One of the greatest problems the project deals with is the inability of many potential project participants to collect, collate, and deliver newspapers to the project location in Indianapolis. Potential participants seem eager to get their newspapers microfilmed, but often are unwilling or unable to follow through with the necessary preliminary work on their newspaper collections. When a local "leader" does not emerge who can contact all potential repositories in the local area, publicize the need to locate old papers in private collections, and deliver the newspapers to Indianapolis, the project director is forced to do the travel and negotiations, which is time-consuming and costly for the project.

Another problem is the recurring rumor that the Indiana Historical Society Newspaper Microfilm Project provides free microfilming for participants. Although the Society does heavily subsidize the cost of microfilming newspapers (over 50% of the cost of filming), free microfilming is not yet a reality. In fact, the Indiana Historical Society believes it is beneficial for participants to share in the cost of producing the microfilm. In many cases, the fund-raising drives and local volunteer efforts in support of newspaper microfilming heighten community spirit and develop an increased awareness about an area's newspaper resources.

An important part of the Newspaper Microfilm Project is the researching of collections in repositories around the state, and there are several considerations for researchers to keep in mind as they investigate newspaper repositories. First, it is necessary to ascertain the hours of the repository to make sure it will be open when the researcher arrives. Many Indiana repositories (especially small libraries, historical societies, and weekly newspaper offices) are only open at certain hours of certain days. It is also important to verify that the individual who actually controls physical access to the papers will be available (e.g., will the person with the key be there?). Occasionally researchers speak to one librarian or curator and are told they can have access to the newspaper collection, only to return later to the same repository and be told by another person that the collection is restricted or missing.

When seeking newspapers at a repository, a person must be prepared to look in all possible locations—newspapers are not always neatly arranged on shelves in bindings. Newspapers have been found stuffed in cardboard boxes with duplicator fluid and other supplies, in grocery sacks near piles of trash, and in every other conceivable location. At other repositories a researcher may be told that no newspapers are available for examination because the librarian or curator may feel the researcher will want to take the papers from the local repository to a central collection in another city. Some repository staff members are suspicious of visits by researchers and genealogists if they have seen materials disappear following earlier visits by such individuals, while other staff members resist the efforts of researchers interested in gathering holdings information by stating that the repository staff just filled out a similar request for information by another agency and "we don't have anything new to add."

Yet, for all the trials involved in researching, processing, and microfilming newspapers, there are few joys that equal the satisfaction of slowing the deterioration and destruction of valuable newspaper sources through preservation microfilming. Newspapers are the best (and sometimes the only) source available for the examination of much of our history, and every possible effort must be exerted to protect this valuable resource.

Working in a Newspaper Reference Collection

Heidi K. Martin

SUMMARY. The Indiana State Library has accumulated the largest collection of Indiana newspapers in existence. The sheer physical size of this collection has necessitated that newspapers be administered separately from other library sources. Collection policies, preservation and storage methods, and reference and access procedures have been specifically developed for the collection. This paper details the policies and procedures employed, and includes some special considerations concerning future growth of the collection.

The newspaper is a document set apart from many library sources by its transient nature, which often promotes an unselfconscious tone. News articles, editorials, vital statistics, syndicated columns and advertising are explicit features of the newspaper. Opinions, social trends and community values are implicitly portrayed. Together, the obvious and the obscure content of the newspaper create the pages of a composite "diary" of a community. The newspaper's unequaled role as a daily logbook makes it crucial for libraries to collect and preserve both historical and current newspapers.

The Indiana State Library early recognized the unique nature of newspapers and the need to devote a separate section to them. In December 1933, after the library had moved into a new building, newspapers were designated as a separate collection of the Division of Indiana History and Archives. By 1937, the newspaper collection had become a section under the care of the newly created Archives Division. Eventually, on June 7, 1943, a full-time staff member was appointed to work in the Newspaper Section.[1] Today the unit, staffed by two librarians and a page, is administered by the State Library's Indi-

---

Heidi K. Martin holds an MS in Library Science and an MA in history from Case Western Reserve University. She has been a newspaper librarian and a field agent and is currently a reference librarian at Indiana State Library, 140 North Senate Avenue, Indianapolis, IN 46204.

ana Division. The goals of the Section are to collect and preserve Indiana newspapers and to provide access to the collection and reference assistance in its use.

The collection, which is the largest of Indiana newspapers in existence, contains items dating back to 1804, when *The Indiana Gazette*, the first newspaper published in Indiana Territory, began appearing. Although Indiana newspapers are the Section's main concern, files of out-of-state historical newspapers and major out-of-state dailies are also maintained. The total holdings of the Section number approximately 3500 titles consisting of an estimated 20,000 bound volumes or packages and 50,000 reels of microfilm.*

COLLECTION POLICY

Agreeing upon the definition of a newspaper is essential in the formulation of a newspaper collection policy. The Library of Congress bases its definition of a newspaper on content and readership rather than on physical medium. The definition reads as follows:

> A newspaper is a serial publication which is designed to be a primary source of written information on current events connected with public affairs, either local, national, and/or international in scope. It contains a broad range of news on all subjects and activities and is not limited to any specific subject matter. It may include (although not primarily) articles on literary or other subjects as well as advertising, legal notices, vital statistics, and illustrations. Newspapers are intended for the general public. The general public may be further qualified and/or limited by 1) geographic location, e.g., local community; and/or 2) ethnic, cultural, racial, political or national group. A newspaper *usually* has the following characteristics: it is originally printed on newsprint; it does not have a cover; it has a masthead; and it has a format of not less than four columns per page.[2]

The Newspaper Section accepts this definition. It does not regard every item printed on newsprint as a newspaper, although most newspapers in the Indiana State Library collection appear on newsprint. A newspaper must represent a definite locality: a county, township, city, college campus, prison, military base, etc. It is generally issued

---

*Editor's Note: As of Spring 1986.

weekly or more frequently, although exceptions exist. A newspaper's readers are not necessarily limited to a specific audience, but the newspaper may be produced with a certain minority or ethnic group in mind (e.g., Hispanic, Polish, Black). On the other hand, the Section does not collect newspapers that represent particular religious denominations. The newspaper should emphasize general news. Physical size does not matter, but Indiana publication is required. Free distribution as well as paid subscription newspapers are considered for inclusion in the collection. Since the Section is part of a division that has a broader collection policy, publications not suited for inclusion as newspapers are considered for and often added to the collections of the Reference Section, Indiana Division.

The Newspaper Section receives every major daily state newspaper in both paper and microfilm formats. Many weekly newspapers are also received in both formats. When microfilm is received, the corresponding paper copies are removed for recycling. Newspapers issued less frequently than weekly are received in paper format only. As the section's budget is not as large as it might be, microfilm subscriptions consume a large portion of available funds. Therefore, in an attempt to acquire for the library as many different newspapers as possible publishers are solicited from time to time for complimentary or reduced-price subscriptions. Microfilm is the format of choice for preservation, but as paper copies meet the expectations of patrons who wish to read the latest news, the staff feels obliged to include both formats in the collection. A breakdown of subscriptions is as follows:

Paper Subscriptions

Out of state	11
In state	
Daily	80
Tri-weekly	3
Bi-weekly	6
Weekly	182
Tri-monthly	1
Monthly	4
Every two months	1
TOTAL	288

Microfilm Subscriptions

Out of state	5
In state	
Daily	60
Weekly	3
TOTAL	68

Newspapers are also received by donation. Donations can take the form of an entire run of a publisher's back files or of a single issue from someone's attic or basement. Everything is accepted, but the right is reserved to keep or discard donations as seems most practical. Less frequently, microfilm donations are received, usually master negatives, from which positive copies are produced for reference use. Additionally, a project established by the Indiana Historical Society in 1980 to microfilm pre-1920 newspapers provides the Section each year with positive copies of hundreds of reels of Indiana newspapers. The Indiana Historical Society also works cooperatively with the Newspaper Section to microfilm current issues of small Indiana town daily, bi-weekly, and weekly newspapers that are not microfilmed commercially. This program annually provides a number of microfilmed newspapers. These are as follows:

Daily	3
Bi-weekly	3
Weekly	36
TOTAL	42

The tasks of the Newspaper Section would be simplified if people automatically donated to it all of their historical newspapers; but since this rarely happens, solicitation must be used as a third method of adding to the collections. Active field agent work was promoted vigorously by the Indiana State Library in the 1960s and 1970s, and this resulted in the addition of many items to the collection. Since then, this effort has lost its momentum, and now keeping contact throughout the state with publishers, librarians and historians is the primary mechanism used to uncover wanted materials.

A crucial facet in the gathering of newspapers, both historical and current, is thorough record-keeping. From 100 to 200 paper subscriptions are received each day, and checked in by date on file cards arranged alphabetically by city. Microfilm reels received by subscription are recorded similarly. The check-in cards allow quick verification as to whether or not a title was received on a particular day, and over time allow for the checking of issues never received or missing. Careful checking is important to ensure that all paper copies that will not later be obtained on microfilm or that will be microfilmed from the Newspaper Section's copies are received issue by issue. This is of the essence, as it seems fated that the one issue missing in a given month or year will be the one that a patron requires. Current newspapers of course quickly become the historical resources of tomorrow. Thus, special emphasis is put on ensuring that current files are as complete as possible. Publishers are contacted for missing issues on a monthly basis, as many small companies do not retain extra copies for more than a month or two. Usually publishers are very cooperative in supplying missing issues.

Recording non-subscription items is accomplished in a different manner. Each acquisition is given an accession number, assigned a storage area, arranged, and as staff time permits, inventoried. Information concerning new items is recorded in an accession register: accession numbers, titles and dates, donors, dates of receipt, and date added to collections are included. The accession register provides a permanent record of non-subscription additions to the collections. (See the proposed procedures in Appendix 1.)

Negative microfilm reel lists, arranged by county, constitute a third major set of records kept by the Newspaper Section. Many master negative microfilm reels controlled by the Indiana State Library are stored with a separate state agency, the Archives Division of the Commission on Public Records. The negative reel lists provide titles, dates, and reel numbers for holdings in the Archives Division, and locations of additional negatives controlled by the Indiana State Library but stored with a commercial microfilmer such as University Microfilms International. In case of damage or loss, the negative reel lists are used to determine the source to go to in replacing a particular title and date. They are used also in meeting requests for purchase of all the newspaper microfilm that can be provided for a certain county or city.

PRESERVATION AND STORAGE

The physical nature of newspapers encourages self-destruction — at least for those produced since the 1880s. Up until the late 1800s newspapers as well as books were printed on high quality rag paper made of pulverized cotton and linen fibers. In the 1850s it was discovered that paper could be made cheaply and in great quantities by the mechanical process of grinding coniferous wood. But it was not until the 1880s, when chemical production was combined with mechanical production to produce superior and more versatile pulp, that woodpulp paper came into wide use.[3] Twentieth century newsprint is composed of a combination of a 75-85% mechanically ground woodpulp and a 15-25% unbleached chemically produced woodpulp. Analysts of the newsprint industry historically have not been concerned with the preservation of newspapers as these ". . . have a very short life, and to achieve a wide circulation they must be printed as economically as possible on cheap, mass produced material."[4] Newsprint composition produces a very acidic paper that quickly becomes brown and brittle. Thus, it has become the responsibility of librarians and conservators to extend the useful life of newspapers.*

Pre-1880s rag paper newspapers still have a long life ahead of them, and so are worth keeping indefinitely. It was common practice up until the late 1940s to bind newspapers at the Indiana State Library. In many cases the practice of binding has effectively preserved the rag newspapers so that they are nearly as white and pliable as when they were produced. In contrast, aged woodpulp newspapers, whether bound or not, are subject to crumbling at the slightest touch.

The enemies of newsprint are numerous: light, humidity, temperature and pollutants in the air. The Indiana State Library houses its collection in a humidity and temperature controlled area, with a halon fire suppressant system. A relatively inexpensive method of preservation for the paper copies is employed: they are flattened with as few folds between two pieces of heavy-weight corrugated cardboard, and wrapped with brown craft paper in two to five inch thick packages. The size of the package is based on an appropriate chronological time span and the thickness of each issue. If particular issues are recognized as bearing extreme historical significance and are in very poor condition, they may be deacidified and encapsulated. Generally, however, newspapers are dealt with on such a massive scale that specialized preservation techniques cannot be provided for individual issues. Paper copies are stored on heavy steel roller shelves arranged from floor to ceiling and spaced so that three or four volumes or bundles fit on a shelf.

***Editor's Note**: Further information on this topic is contained in the article by Thomas D. Lund.

Currently, microfilm is the most useful and most widely used technology available to libraries for the preservation of newspapers. This is a medium in an affordable price range, and one that is portable both for in-house use and for transportation through interlibrary loan. With the help of the Indiana Historical Society, the Indiana State Library is slowly but steadily transferring many of its nineteenth and early twentieth century newspaper files onto microfilm. The master negative copies are stored separately from the positive reference copies in a climate controlled, fireproof vault. Substituting microfilm for paper copies allows provision of assistance to researchers in a less apprehensive manner, for although the originals cannot be replaced if they are lost or damaged, duplicates of microfilm can be made.

REFERENCE AND ACCESS

The Newspaper Section serves patrons in several ways: in person, by telephone call, by letter, and through interlibrary loan. The Section's users are divided nearly evenly between state government staff and the general public. Interlibrary loan requests are increasingly more frequent, as the Section's holdings are gradually being entered into the Online Computer Library Center (OCLC) database by the Indiana Newspaper Project staff and as new titles are microfilmed and received from the Indiana Historical Society Newspaper Microfilming Project. The Newspaper Section has a very liberal interlibrary loan policy insofar as microfilm is concerned — if an item is in the collection, it can be loaned — whereas many Indiana public libraries will not allow their microfilm to leave the building. Thus, the State Library provides a valuable service not only to in-state libraries but also to researchers around the country who might not otherwise have access to Indiana newspapers.

Reference work in the Newspaper Section is markedly different from that provided in other public service areas of the library. The reference service required appears quite routine, since generally patrons request newspapers by place — city, township, or county — and date. It is simple enough to retrieve an appropriately labelled volume or reel of microfilm. More is needed, however, than this. Proper service can be provided only after time has been spent working with the reference sources. A knowledge of the different types of coverage provided by a daily as opposed to a weekly newspaper, of where to look for obituaries in a given decade, and of the political tendencies of different newspapers in a county (one called *The Democrat* could be Republican in philosophy) may be possessed by a person who knows the object of his or her search, but if that person is confused by the format of the reference sources used to locate the material, his or her knowledge will be of little use. A thorough grounding in the geography of the state is also an essential qualification for the newspaper librarian. Familiarity with the history of the state, and a general knowledge of American, local, and world history are also helpful. Unlike most reference sources, newspapers are not usually self-indexed. A 1986 issue of the *Indianapolis News* is different in format from one published in 1886. The newspaper librarian who is familiar with the content and format of newspapers can consequently save valuable time for the patron by suggesting search strategies likely to prove effective.

Reference requests usually take one of several different forms: requests for current news; obituaries and other vital statistics; historical or social information on a specific topic; and exhibit materials. As stated earlier, patrons generally have a specific date and locality in mind when they enter a request. Current news is requested most often by state government offices and local businesses. A state legislator may send over a staff member to peruse the current month's newspapers from his or her constituency or to examine recent articles in the *New York Times* or *Wall Street Journal* concerning a federal ruling that affects Indiana. In like fashion, a local contractor, trying to justify slow progress in constructing a downtown office building, might have an employee come to photocopy recent weather reports from an Indianapolis newspaper.

Genealogists make up perhaps the most numerous group of Newspaper Section patrons. Obtaining obituaries is their primary objective, although occasionally they are searching for marriage, birth, or adoption notices. Often genealogists will have previously visited court houses, and so bring copies of death and marriage certificates to use in searching State Library holdings for clues concerning family relationships.

Researchers investigating a particular historical or social issue are a third group of patrons. Examples of specific topics where newspapers have been helpful are: the frequency of tornadoes in the Midwest; the history of the Monon Railroad; and a composite list of coaching records in Indiana high schools. There is no question but that newspapers are to such persons a vital primary source of material in their research efforts.

A fourth type of request is for the use of newspapers for display or publication purposes. Indianapolis city museums and the state historical society frequently request original newspapers for use in exhibits or to be photographed, duplicated, and used as handouts. Local television stations sometimes request our assistance in retrieving a paper copy or bound volume with an especially graphic front page story. For example, during the 1986 visit of Halley's Comet a local television station videotaped and aired a segment on its news program in which was used an original 1910 issue of the *Indianapolis Star* containing articles about the sighting of Halley's Comet and the concurrent death of Mark Twain. Such uses pinpoint the need to retain at least some original paper copies, and not to transfer holdings entirely to microfilm.

Newspaper librarians, as other librarians, face a problem that was not noticeably present a few decades ago—the I-have-to-take-it-with-me syndrome. Whereas patrons were once content to hand-copy an article from a newspaper, now they ask for photocopies. The problem is solved by purchasing a reader-printer. As user-operated machines have been deemed inappropriate in this context, in the Indiana State Library Newspaper Section, staff members produce whatever copies the users need. Bound volumes and badly deteriorating original copies must of course be treated carefully. Sometimes these are not able to withstand the strain that photocopying imposes, and so each request for copying is handled individually. The ultimate decision is based on the condition of the newspaper. There must be a constant balancing of the patron's wishes against the responsibility to preserve resources for coming generations.

The Indiana State Library has a closed stack policy. For this reason, the user has no opportunity to browse and must rely on printed guides to the holdings. Although the library's newspapers were not cataloged in the past, several inventories of holdings have been produced over the years—a card file, a set of looseleaf volumes listing holdings issue by issue, and the recently published *Indiana Newspaper Bibliography* by John W. Miller. All guides, are arranged alphabetically by county, city, title, and chronology. They vary in detail and accuracy, and reliance is placed on all of them and on the memory of the staff in verifying holdings. Additions and deletions are recorded in the most recent bibliography. The Indiana Newspaper Project represents an initial effort to formally catalog the Indiana State Library's newspapers. The newly-created catalog records and the State Library and Indiana Historical Society holdings are being transferred into the OCLC database. Soon the staff should be able to access all State Library newspaper holdings by title and date in the OCLC database. The catalog records are also being transferred to the Indiana State Library's online catalog. Each effort to improve the "catalog" of holdings has been spurred by the need to respond more rapidly and effectively than previously possible to user requests.

With a growing public awareness of the research value of newspapers have come increased user expectations, one of which is indexing of the content of the newspapers. In the Section's holdings are several newspaper indexes, most of which are card files produced by volunteers or by the Works Progress Administration (WPA) in the 1930s. A few others are bound volumes produced by private researchers and still others are microfilmed card files. The indexes vary in thoroughness and focus: some emphasize births, deaths and marriages, while others are subject-oriented. Each index is keyed to a specific Indiana location. The Indiana State Library employs one full-time librarian to index Indiana-related materials in the two daily Indianapolis newspapers and to add subject entries to a card file that dates back to 1898. This newspaper index is a major reference tool for both librarians and patrons, and currently accounts for a majority of the reference requests in the Newspaper Section. While it is unquestionably a worthwhile pursuit, newspaper indexing requires enormous amounts of time. The Newspaper Section staff is currently concentrating its efforts on collecting and preserving Indiana newspapers. The hope of course is that these will be indexed at a later date.

Though Indiana State Library users are principally interested in Indiana newspapers, users occasionally request out-of-state newspapers. For this reason, a reference shelf is kept of bibliographies and guides to newspaper holdings in other states and to special subject newspapers such as those directed to a Black or ethnic audience. Standard newspaper reference sources including *The IMS Directory of Publications, Newspapers in Microform*, and *American Newspapers 1821-1936*, are also held.

PLANNING FOR THE FUTURE

Up to the present the Indiana State Library Newspaper Section has been able to collect an unlimited number of newspapers, but space for bound and wrapped paper copies is now at a premium. In such a situation, it is necessary to "weed" the collections. Now whenever microfilm is received for a newspaper that is also held in pulp paper copy, the paper copies are removed from the collection. Because of their longevity, all rag paper copies are retained, regardless of whether or not they are microfilmed. If possible, newspapers removed from the collection are donated for indexing and clipping to an appropriate library or historical society. A deaccession register is kept in which are noted the items removed and the date and place of their disposition. (See the proposed procedures in Appendix 2.)

It is clear that weeding files of older newspapers that have been microfilmed will not entirely solve space problems. A newspaper collection is not static; current subscriptions arrive every day. Most daily newspapers are commercially microfilmed, but many less frequently published newspapers are not. The Library of Congress warns that "A changing technology and a changing economy may result in more and more periodicals and other newspaper serials being published on newsprint as well as newspapers being published solely in microform or other physical media such as mimeograph copy, xerox copy, etc."[5] Thus, it is important to recognize that defining what is or is not a newspaper constitutes an ongoing process. It is the newspaper librarian's task to assess the validity of collecting and preserving the "shopper" newspaper, the neighborhood tabloid and other such publications that some consider newspapers and some do not. It is not always possible to react positively to past choices and definitions. By evaluating and choosing which newspapers to collect and by preserving these on microfilm soon after their publication the librarian makes a specific and, it can be hoped, worthwhile commitment to the future.

The Indiana State Library Newspaper Section is actually a special library, one with the purpose of offering its users the full gamut of the news, from accounts of nineteenth century occurrences now defined as history to today's late-breaking stories. It is the staff's responsibility to preserve today's page in the diary of each Indiana community and to add this page to all the earlier ones.

NOTES

1. Indiana State Library. *Annual Report of the Library and Historical Divisions of the State of Indiana For the Fiscal Year Ending June 30, 1934* (Indianapolis: Wm. B. Burford Printing Co., 1934), p. 12; Indiana State Library. *Annual Report of the Indiana State Library For the Fiscal Year Ending June 30, 1937* (Fort Wayne: Fort Wayne Printing Co., 1937), p. 6; Indiana State Library. *Annual Report of the Indiana State Library of the State of Indiana For the Fiscal Year Ending June 30, 1943* (Indianapolis: Bookwalter-Ball-Greathouse Printing Co., 1943), p. 1.

2. Harriman, Robert. *Newspaper Cataloging Manual: CONSER/USNP Edition* (Washington, D.C. : Serials Record Division, Library of Congress, 1984), p. 2.

3. Intelligence Unit of "The Economist." *Paper For Printing Today and Tomorrow. Press, Film and Radio in the World Today.* (Paris: Unesco, 1952), p. 16.

4. Intelligence Unit of "The Economist." *The Problem of Newsprint and Other Printing Paper*. (Paris: Unesco, 1949), p. 37.

5. New York State Library. "Conference on Newspaper Bibliography and Preservation" Summary of Proceedings Held at Cultural Education Center May 4, 1979 (Albany: New York State Library, 1979), Mimeographed, Appendix XIII, p. 53.

APPENDIX I.
ACCESSION PROCEDURES (proposed)
Newspaper Section, Indiana Division, Indiana State Library

INTRODUCTION

Periodically, the Newspaper Section receives both paper and microfilmed newspapers <u>other than</u> by subscription. These donations or purchases can take the <u>form of single</u> issues, several year's worth of a newspaper title, or any amount in between. Newspapers can be acquired from private individuals or institutions; currently we receive a large amount of donated newspaper microfilm from the Indiana Historical Society Newspaper Microfilm Project. These procedures are intended to provide a mechanism of accounting for all non-subscription paper and microfilm additions from the time they enter the building until they are added to the collections. The accession register produced will create a permanent record of additions to the collection.

1. Each acquisition should be given a temporary number, which will be used to keep track of the item or group of items until it is added to the collections. The temporary accession number should also be recorded in the accession register. Accession numbers consist of the last two digits of the calendar year, a dash, and a sequential number. If several cities and/or titles are represented, they should all have the same number, but should be listed separately in the accession register. Each acquisition, no matter if it is only one issue of a newspaper, will be numbered. This should be a cursory inventory of what is in the accession, giving beginning and ending dates. See the sample accession sheet following.

2. The accession number should be placed on the outside wrappers, boxes or containers of each accession, and all items in an accession should be stored together. The number should <u>not</u> be placed on the items themselves.

3. As time permits, a staff member will conduct a thorough inventory of each accession. Only one accession, whether it consists of an item or a group of items, per staff member should be inventoried at one time.

4. Integration into the collection follows the inventory. The accession will be added to the State Library's collections according to the following guidelines:

PAPER COPIES

    A. Where more than one "rag"* paper copy exists they may both be kept in the collection. Where more than one "pulp"* paper copy exists, only the one in the best condition will be kept.

    B. No "pulp" copies will be added where the issue exists on positive microfilm at the State Library. "Rag" copies will be kept in addition to microfilm.**

    C. Wherever possible, single copy additions to the collection will be made in existing loose bundles. Where only bound volumes exist in the State Library's collection, single issues from an accession will be added to the "miscellaneous" files.

MICROFILM COPIES

    A. For many of the microfilm reels in the collection, the master negatives are held in the vault of the Archives Division, Commission on Public Records. Each master negative is numbered and the corresponding positive in the Newspaper Section collection has the same number. Lists of negatives held in the Archives vault are kept in the Newspaper Section files and are arranged by county. Other locations for newspaper microfilm master negatives owned by the Indiana State Library include: University Microfilms International, Bell and Howell Micro Photo Division

APPENDIX I (continued)

(these two companies combined in December 1985) and the University of Chicago (we share in the cost and ownership of the master negative for the Kentland <u>Newton County Enterprise</u>). ***

B. Any new negatives or negative/positive combinations added to the collection should receive a permanent number. Microfilm received from the Indiana Historical Society Newspaper Microfilm Project is already numbered. Microfilm received from commercial sources should be coded in this manner: C for commercial, the first two letters of the county represented, the last two digits of the calendar year, and a sequential number (i.e. Columbus, IN, Bartholomew County miscellaneous, two reels received in 1986 from the Frederic Luther Co. would be C-Ba-86-1 and C-Ba-86-2). See the county abbreviations list attached.

C. The counties, cities, titles dates and reel numbers should be recorded in the Newspaper Section's negatives holdings files.

D. If two microfilm reels reflect the same titles and dates, but were filmed at different times and/or by different operations (i.e. the reels are not identical), both reels will be integrated into the collections. If two or more reels are identical, only one will be retained in the collection and the other(s) will be placed in a duplicate file.

5. Upon completion of the inventory and integration of the accession, the staff member will date and initial the accession register.

6. Any additions representing new titles or dates will be recorded in the appropriate written holdings guides, and/or on-line catalog (if the maintenance of the OCLC newspaper catalog records becomes the responsibility of the Newspaper Section).

7. Staff members will notify personnel of the Indiana Newspaper Project each time an accession has been inventoried and integrated into the collections.

---

* "Rag" paper denotes a better quality paper which is off-white or white in color. "Pulp" paper is a very acidic wood pulp paper, characterized by a brown color and brittle texture. Generally publishers ceased to use 100% rag paper in the early 1880s; in the late 1880s newsprint was often a mixture of rag and pulp, and so is slightly acidic. By the 1890s most newspapers had adopted the use of very acidic pulp paper. In the interest of maintaining a fixed date for the holdings of all newspaper titles, and to ensure the retention of nearly all rag paper copies, the Newspaper Section will retain all original newspapers through 1885. <u>The definition of "rag", as used in these procedures, will mean all original newspapers through 1885.</u>

** The exception to this rule is that all Indianapolis newspapers are retained in both formats whenever they exist.

*** Other locations for microfilmed Indiana newspaper master negatives <u>not owned</u> by the Indiana State Library include:

Bell and Howell, Micro Photo Division, Wooster, OH
Forman Company, Monmouth, IL
Morrow Microfilm
Notre Dame University, South Bend, IN
University Microfilms International, Ann Arbor, MI
University of Chicago Phtocuplication Department, Chicago, IL

Depauw University, Greencastle, IN
Hanover College, Hanover, IN
Lebanon Public Library, Lebanon, IN
New Albany Public Library, New Albany, IN
Willard Library, Evansville, IN
other libraries and publishers across the state

APPENDIX I (continued)

ACCESSION REGISTER

Newspaper Section, Indiana Division, Indiana State Library

(5/86 HM)

Number	Date rec'd and staff member	Newspaper title and dates	Number and type of item (bound, wrapped, single, microfilm)	Donor and complete address	Added to collections (date, staff)
86-1	1-29-86 H.M.	Frankfort Times Jan. 5, 1890	1 single issue	John Smith 1250 St. Paul Dr. Corydon, IN 00000	2-15-86 H.M.
86-2	2-1-86 H.M.	Beech Grove, IN Perry Township Weekly 1936-1977	15 boxes of folded papers	Mary Martin, publisher 1000 David St. Indianapolis, IN 00000	3-10-86 J.S.
86-3	3-2-86 J.S.	Columbus, IN Bartholomew County Miscellaneous Microfilm Reel 1840-1896 #C-Ba-86-1	one negative reel, filmed by Frederic Luther Company	Robert Cook 20 Sunrise Drive Capitola, CA 00000	3-6-86 J.S. positive copy made and added. 3-8-86 neg. sent to Archives vault.

APPENDIX I (continued)

INDIANA COUNTY ABBREVIATIONS

County	Abbreviation
Adams	Ad
Allen	Al
Bartholomew	Ba
Benton	Be
Blackford	Bl
Boone	Bo
Brown	Br
Carroll	C
Cass	Ca
Clark	Ck
Clay	Cl
Clinton	Clt
Crawford	Cr
Daviess	Da
Dearborn	Db
Decatur	Dc
DeKalb	DeK
Delaware	DeL
Dubois	Du
Elkhart	El
Fayette	Fa
Floyd	Fl
Fountain	Fo
Franklin	Fr
Fulton	Fu
Gibson	Gi
Grant	Gn
Greene	Gr
Hamilton	H
Hancock	Han
Harrison	Har
Hendricks	He
Henry	Hn

APPENDIX I (continued)

County	Abbreviation
Howard	Ho
Huntington	Hu
Jackson	Ja
Jasper	Jas
Jay	Jay
Jefferson	Je
Jenninngs	Jn
Johnson	Jo
Knox	Kn
Kosciusko	Ko
LaGrange	L
Lake	La
LaPorte	Lp
Lawrence	Lw
Madison	M
Marion	Ma
Marshall	Mars
Martin	Mart
Miami	Mi
Monroe	Mo
Montgomery	Mon
Morgan	Mr
Newton	N
Noble	No
Ohio	Oh
Orange	Or
Owen	Ow
Parke	Pa
Perry	Pe
Pike	Pi
Porter	Po
Posey	Pos
Pulaski	Pu
Putnam	Put
Randolph	Ra
Ripley	Ri
Rush	Ru

APPENDIX I (continued)

County	Abbreviation
St. Joseph	S
Scott	Sc
Shelby	Sh
Spencer	Sp
Starke	St
Steuben	Ste
Sullivan	Su
Switzerland	Sw
Tippecanoe	T
Tipton	Ti
Union	Un
Vanderburgh	Va
Vermillion	Ve
Vigo	Vi
Wabash	Wab
Warren	Wan
Warrick	War
Washington	Was
Wayne	Way
Wells	We
White	Wh
Whitley	Whi

APPENDIX II.

DEACCESSION PROCEDURES (proposed)

Newspaper Section, Indiana Division, Indiana State Library

INTRODUCTION

Although one purpose of the Newspaper Section is to collect and preserve Indiana newspapers, at times both paper and microfilm copies may be removed, or deaccessioned, from the collection. Microfilm will rarely be deaccessioned, but paper copies will regularly be removed from the collections upon replacement by microfilm. Weeding the collections due to lack of storage space may also precipitate the removal of paper copies. All deaccessions will be performed according to the following guidelines.

1. "Pulp" * newspapers which are received on microfilm will be removed from the collection. "Rag" * paper copy newspapers received on microfilm will be retained. **

2. When current subscription commercial microfilm is received, the paper copies will be removed from the collections. At this time, the bagged paper copies are removed for recycling by Mr. and Mrs. Hopkins of Anderson, Indiana.

APPENDIX II (continued)

DEACCESSION PROCEDURES, continued

3. Procedures relating to microfilm received from the Indiana Historical Society Newspaper Microfilm Project (IHSNMP):

   A. Periodically the IHSNMP removes portions of our collections to be microfilmed. Usually our copies are integrated with those of some other Indiana library or historical society.

   B. After our paper copies are microfilmed, the Director of IHSNMP may deliver <u>any State Library owned post-1885</u> copies to the participating library or institution which is interested in having them for their files, or for clipping and indexing. The Director of IHSNMP will provide the Newspaper Section and the Indiana Newspaper Project with specific lists of what has been transferred to another institution. If the participating institution does not want the paper copies, they will be placed on designated shelving units for papers that have been filmed, and they will not be integrated back into the collection. The staff of the IHSNMP will return <u>any State Library owned pre-1886</u> papers to their original location in the Newspaper Section stack area.

   C. Concerning the "update" microfilming of the past year's newspapers (currently conducted annually by the IHSNMP in conjunction with the Indiana State Library), State Library newspaper copies which have been microfilmed will either be given to the institution participating in the program, or will be discarded three months after filming. This three month period will allow the original newspapers to be refilmed if there are problems with the microfilm.

   D. All expediency will be used in properly weeding and refiling newspapers which have been microfilmed.

4. A Newspaper Librarian will contact Indiana institutions which have not participated in microfilming, to determine if someone is interested in utilizing the "pulp" microfilmed newspapers set aside after microfilming. A concerted effort will be made to place these newspapers with another institution. However, based on space considerations, if no interest is generated, the accumulated "pulp" newspapers will be periodically discarded.

5. All issues and/or bound volumes removed from the collection will be deleted from the appropriate written holdings guides, and/or on-line catalog (if the maintenance of the OCLC newspaper catalog records becomes the responsibility of the Newspaper Section).

6. Upon completion of a deaccession, or upon notification by the IHSNMP that certain files have been transferred to another institution, a staff member will record the transaction in the deaccession register. The deaccession register will be subdivided into twenty-six alphabetical parts, each containing, in chronological order, all deaccessions for cities beginning with a particular letter. See the sample deaccession sheet following.

7. Staff members will notify personnel of the Indiana Newspaper Project each time any newspapers are removed from the collection (transferred to another institution or discarded), other than the routine discarding of "pulp" newspapers for which we have received "update" microfilm or commercial microfilm.

---

* "Rag" paper denotes a better quality paper which is off-white or white in color. "Pulp" paper is a very acidic wood pulp paper, characterized by a brown color and brittle texture. Generally publishers ceased to use 100% rag paper in the early 1880s; in the late 1880s newsprint was often a mixture of rag and pulp, and so is slightly acidic. By the 1890s most newspapers had adopted the use of very acidic pulp paper. In the interest

APPENDIX II (continued)

DEACCESSION PROCEDURES, continued

of maintaining a fixed date for the holdings of all newspaper titles, and to ensure the retention of nearly all rag paper copies, the Newspaper Section will retain all original newspapers through 1885. <u>The definition of "rag", as used in these procedures, will mean all original newspapers through 1885.</u>

** The exception to this rule is that all Indianapolis newspapers are retained in both formats whenever they exist.

APPENDIX II (continued)

DEACCESSION REGISTER
Newspaper Section, Indiana Division, Indiana State Library

(5/86 HM)

City, Newspaper title and dates	Number and type of item (bound, wrapped, single, microfilm)	Transferred to: (institution, person, address)	Date removed & staff
Knox, IN *Knox Leader* 1979-1983	10 wrapped bundles	Starke County Public Library Steve Chilcoate 100 Main Street Knox, IN 00000	3-17-86 H.M.
Knox, IN *Knox Leader* July - December 1980	1 microfilm neg. reel, transferred from Archives vault	Knox Leader, publisher 50 Major Street Knox, In 00000	4-6-86 H.M.
Kendallville, IN *News-Sun* 1888, 1890, 1911-1915, 1920-21, Aug. 1922-1930	2 bound volumes, 25 wrapped bundles	Noble County Historical Society Bill Whitacre 12 Washington Kendallville, IN 00000	4-7-86 H.M.

Newspaper Collections at the Center for Research Libraries

Karla D. Petersen
Ray Boylan

SUMMARY. Newspapers play a significant role in research in a number of fields, but because of problems in acquiring, storing and providing access to them, they are not as widely available as needed. In this paper the authors discuss the history of the newspaper collections at the Center for Research Libraries, the special problems in collecting and handling newspapers, the Center's participation in the National Endowment for the Humanities' U.S. Newspaper Program, and newspaper preservation. They point out that preservation efforts at CRL and elsewhere are not enough, and that much more must be done to assure the continued existence of these valuable resources.

Since its inception as the Midwest Inter-Library Center, newspapers have been one of the primary types of material with which the Center for Research Libraries (CRL) has been concerned. CRL's collections are intended to supplement and complement the major collections in North American libraries. Newspapers have several characteristics that make them an important part of this kind of collection.

Newspapers form an essential resource for historical research in a number of fields. Because of their bulk, however, it is expensive for research libraries to maintain significant backfiles, and the backfiles that are maintained are soon in need of preservation work. Microfilm editions of major U.S. newspapers are available; but because they are costly, most libraries are able to collect microfilm files only of highly important national newspapers and of others of specifically regional interest. Foreign newspapers, with the exception of a few major titles, are rarely held in North American libraries. To be sure, most research

---

Karla D. Petersen is director, Technical Services Division, The Center for Research Libraries, 6050 S. Kenwood Avenue, Chicago, IL 60637. She has an MS in Library Science from the University of Minnesota.

Ray Boylan is director, Collection Resources, The Center for Research Libraries, 6050 S. Kenwood Avenue, Chicago, IL 60637.

libraries maintain subscriptions for current awareness use to a limited number of foreign newspapers, but few attempt to maintain significant backfiles. Access to retrospective microfilm files of newspapers through interlibrary loan is normally limited. Many libraries will not lend newspapers, and those that do normally restrict the number of reels they will lend at one time.

The primary goal of the Center's policies covering newspapers is to provide long-term access, as opposed to meeting current awareness needs. The Center acquires newspaper files both by way of purchase and by way of deposit by members. With a few exceptions, purchases are limited to microfilm editions. The Center's collection policies divide newspapers into three groups: U.S. general circulation newspapers, U.S. ethnic newspapers, and foreign newspapers.

Subscription to the microfilm editions of current U.S. general circulation newspapers was one of the first acquisitions expenditures approved by the Center's Board of Directors. This took place in 1951; and in 1966 the Board of Directors approved a major expansion of the Center's collection of U.S. general circulation newspapers. The current policy, which is basically a revision and clarification of the 1966 policy, was instituted in 1984.

CRL requires the microfilm editions of general circulation U.S. newspapers in order to ensure nationwide coverage in its collections. Subscriptions are maintained to at least one newspaper from each state, in most — but not all — cases from the state's largest city, with the addition of newspapers from the largest twenty-five cities or metropolitan areas in the nation, ranked according to population. Individual titles are selected on the basis of their availability on microfilm and the quality of their coverage. Newspapers with wide national distribution are excluded. The titles presently excluded on this basis are: the *Christian Science Monitor*, the *New York Times*, *U.S.A. Today*, the *Wall Street Journal*, and the *Washington Post*. The list of titles to which subscriptions are maintained is reviewed every five years. The Center currently has subscriptions to the microfilm editions of sixty-two U.S. general circulation newspapers. To the extent that funds permit, retrospective files of newspapers to which current subscriptions are maintained, or the files of predecessor titles, are acquired with the goal of providing the greatest possible overall national coverage.

Obtaining ethnic newspapers published in the United States is another important aspect of the Center's activities. The Center has a collection of over 500 ethnic titles published in thirty-eight languages. These files cover a period from the early 20th century to the present. In many cases the files are very extensive and, for a significant number of titles, are either the only files or the longest and most complete files now known. The core of this collection was deposited with CRL by the University of Illinois at Urbana-Champaign. In 1917, the University of Illinois began a major effort to collect ethnic newspapers from throughout the United States. Subscriptions were maintained until the early 1950s, when the entire collection, including backfiles of discontinued titles, was deposited with the Center. Over the years, additional backfiles have been added through deposits by other members of the Center. These ethnic newspapers are the focus of much of CRL's preservation effort. The Center also maintains current subscriptions to fifty-two U.S. ethnic newspapers and to ten newspapers intended primarily for Black communities.

CRL began entering subscriptions to foreign newspapers in 1952. In 1956 the Association of Research Libraries (ARL) began the Foreign Newspaper Microfilm Project (FNMP) to provide worldwide coverage of representative foreign titles. From its inception, this project has been administered by CRL and its materials housed there. When appropriate, FNMP enters a subscription to the microfilm edition of a wanted title. If no microfilm edition is available, the project acquires newsprint and does its own filming. The project is supported by annual fees paid by those institutions that wish to participate. Participation allows institutions to borrow any title held by the project, and to purchase at the cost of printing positive reels of titles filmed by the project. From 1956 through 1981, FNMP was owned by ARL and administered by CRL. In 1982 ownership was transferred to the Center, but the project continues to be restricted to institutions paying an annual subscription fee. FNMP currently maintains a representative pool of 113 current foreign newspaper titles. Of these, FNMP does original microfilming of forty-nine titles. FNMP's filming activities have always been coordinated with the filming activities of the Library of Congress.

The Center, in support of area study collection work, also maintains a number of subscriptions to microfilm editions of foreign newspaper titles. These are mostly secondary papers in the countries in which they are published. Countries currently represented are: Egypt, India, Indonesia, Israel, Nepal, Pakistan, Poland, Sri Lanka, and Yugoslavia. At present 149 titles are being received from these countries, of which sixty come from India. Microfilm editions of most are purchased from the Library of Congress.

In addition to the titles acquired under current policies, the Center holds backfiles of a large number of other titles, both domestic and foreign. Many of these are newsprint editions deposited by member libraries. These occupy an entire floor in one of the Center's buildings, and are estimated to number about 30,000 volumes. From 1968 through 1984 it was the Center's policy to attempt to acquire a microform run of any newspaper, domestic or foreign, requested for research purposes by a patron at a member institution. While this policy provided a valuable service to researchers, it also led to a rather fragmented collection. In 1985 the policy was modified to limit such purchases on demand to the backfiles of titles to which a current subscription is being maintained or to a predecessor title from the same city or region. As a result of both current and past acquisition policies, CRL holds over 50,000 reels of newspapers on microfilm.

The Center for Research Libraries' loan policies tend to be much more liberal than normal interlibrary loan practices allow. They are specifically formulated to recognize the fact that the collection consists of material that will be infrequently used and that the normal user is a scholar or graduate student engaged in in-depth research. These more liberal policies are especially important in the case of newspapers, since most institutions place strict limitations on the lending of newspapers in microform. The material borrowed from CRL may be kept for as long as needed by the patron, subject to recall only to fill a request from another institution. A library borrowing more recent issues of a newspaper may have up to twelve reels of microfilm of a particular title per patron at a time. In the case of older backfiles, no limit is placed on the number of reels that may be borrowed at one time. CRL is one of few institutions that will lend newsprint to fill a request. If the requested file proves to be too fragile to lend, CRL will either film it or obtain a film copy to fill the request. Researchers from member institutions can, of course, come to the Center to work with a particular title on site.

Newspapers account for about 13% of the requests filled by CRL. In fiscal year 1985 (July 1984-June 1985), it is estimated that the Center filled approximately 3,200 requests for newspapers. Use studies have indicated that requested newspapers tend to be evenly distributed between domestic and foreign titles. A study of 269 newspaper requests filled in early 1983 revealed that while 65% required four or fewer reels of microfilm to fill, the mean number of reels per filled request was seven. Twenty-four of the requests in this sample required over fifty reels of microfilm to fill.

TECHNICAL PROCESSING

Newspapers present special problems in technical processing to the libraries that collect them. They are expensive and often difficult to acquire; they are time-consuming and expensive to catalog; and they are bulky and fragile in their original format. Further, all of these problems are multiplied when one is dealing with foreign newspapers, as CRL does. CRL acquires newspapers in both microform and original format. Those in hard copy are collected for the purpose of microfilming to provide long term access to this body of material.

The difficulties in the acquisition of foreign newspapers in hard copy are many. It is often difficult, for instance, to maintain subscriptions to newspapers, particularly from Third World countries. A change in government can cause publishing interruptions or cessations, delays in mail service, etc. Issues are often damaged or lost in transport, and claims may go unfilled for long periods of time, if they are ever filled. When a library's primary purpose in collecting these newspapers is for preservation microfilming, it is especially important that files be complete and undamaged. In the case of many foreign newspapers, however, few other libraries in this country maintain subscriptions; and as the subscriptions these libraries have are also unreliable, it becomes very hard to locate and borrow issues from another library to fill in gaps in CRL files.

The acquisition of newspaper files in microform is generally much simpler than their acquisition in hard copy, since many domestic newspapers, especially, are available from large commercial microfilmers. Microforms are, however, very costly, especially if the goal is to maintain not only a current collection, but also substantial backfiles.

Ensuring bibliographic access to newspapers is another important aspect of their processing. Many libraries do not catalog their newspaper holdings, but provide some other means of access: by title on the shelves, by check-in records, etc. At the Center newspapers have always been cataloged, although the standards for cataloging have changed considerably over the years. Early records contained little detail and often had compressed holdings statements with an indication that the holdings were incomplete, but with no indication of how incomplete.

Although the physical description of newspapers in most cases is not as complex as that of other types of serial publication, changes in the masthead design, "minor" changes in title, such as the addition or deletion of a word like "daily," and other similar problems often complicate the cataloging process. The major cataloging difficulty, however, is found in dealing with holdings. Collating newspaper runs in either hard copy or microform is tedious and time-consuming. Further, this is frequently complicated by irregularities in numbering and dates—problems that are most common in foreign titles and domestic ethnic titles. Experience at CRL has shown that catalog records without complete and detailed holdings statements are of little use to those who want to use newspapers, and so full and accurate collation, however expensive, is essential.

Procedures for cataloging newspapers at the Center changed most noticeably when the Center became a participant in the National Endowment for the Humanities U.S. Newspaper Program (USNP) in 1982. CRL was one of the six initial repository libraries, and as such, was involved with the other repositories, the Library of Congress and OCLC in the establishment of the procedures and rules that now govern newspaper cataloging. The *Newspaper Cataloging Manual* is now available from LC, and should be used in all newspaper cataloging. The rules acknowledge the differences between newspapers and other serial publications, and provide for special descriptive elements and access points related specifically to the ways in which newspapers are sought and used.

The libraries that are part of the USNP have CONSER authorization for U.S. newspapers, and the bibliographic records they create go into the CONSER database. With CONSER authorization, permanent changes can be made to the master records on OCLC. While this greatly simplifies the process of upgrading or correcting errors in bibliographic records, it also imposes a large responsibility on the libraries that are doing this work. Record quality is a very real concern, because CONSER records are distributed by LC to networks and other libraries. Catalogers must be very careful to verify fully any changes to be made to existing records, especially if these changes result in the deletion of information from records. Once the change is made, what was there beforehand is gone. CRL's staff frequently contact the original cataloging library about a proposed change before making it. Other catalogers must take the same care in verifying information for original records.

Newspapers are primary source materials for information on cities, counties and regions. Because of this, users often look for newspapers from a certain locale rather than for specific newspaper titles. Before the USNP began operation, access to papers by place had to be provided through devices such as place cross-references in local catalogs. Now, however, a new added entry access point is available for newspapers—the 752 field. This field in the MARC-S format provides access through the place(s) of publication of each paper. Not only does this allow users to find individual papers by place, but it also allows all newspapers from a particular place to be located together in catalogs, union lists, etc.

Another need of the newspaper user is to have holdings statements at the day-specific level, as the user may have need of newspapers published on a specific day. Moreover, the date of publication is more important in access than the issue number. The formats for recording holdings statements in online union lists that were in use at the time the USNP began allowed holdings to be recorded only at the level of year and month. Therefore, a format that allowed for the recording of day-specific holdings was developed by project participants, LC and OCLC, and is being used on the OCLC system in the USNP Union List (NEPU). Another deviation from the normal holdings statement for serials that was allowed for newspapers and prescribed for the USNP was the recording of all holdings, no matter how scattered. The fragile nature of newspapers makes it important for a library to record all of its holdings, not just those weeks, months or years for which most of the issues are held. In some cases, a few scattered issues may be all that is extant of a title; in others, the few issues held may be what are needed to fill in gaps in a run for preservation filming.

PRESERVATION

Preservation of newspapers is a critical concern today. The papers published within the last 100 years or so on acidic chemical pulp paper are rapidly deteriorating. In fact, many titles have disappeared, and are now known only through reference to them in bibliographies. Many others are in imminent danger of being lost. Through programs such as the USNP adequate bibliographic access to newspapers is becoming a reality. Once located, however, newspapers cannot withstand much use. Their preservation is imperative if users are to have access to them in the future. (USNP is now beginning to fund preservation projects for newspapers.)

The Center has worked to preserve newspapers since its early days. CRL has cooperated in this work with a number of institutions, such as the Immigration History Research Center at the University of Minnesota, the Balch Institute in Philadelphia, the New York Public Library and the Library of Congress. Significant assistance in these efforts has come from national funding agencies and ethnic organizations. Through such programs as the Foreign Newspaper Microfilm Project and through other cooperative projects, thousands of reels of newspaper microfilm have been made. CRL has also, within the limits of its budget, filmed brittle materials, but this has been confined primarily to the filming of requested titles that cannot circulate because of their condition. However, neither CRL's efforts nor anyone else's have been enough to stop the loss resulting from deterioration. In an attempt to increase the amount of preservation work being undertaken, the Center is now starting to preserve its U.S. ethnic newspapers under an HEA Title II-C funded project.

The focus of this project is on titles published for the groups from central, eastern and southern Europe that emigrated to the United States in the late 19th and early 20th centuries. There are 241 titles at CRL that fall into the eligible group, and of these 151 need to be filmed. Attempts are being made to fill gaps and complete runs by adding the first or last years of a title to the runs held. Titles are being selected on the basis of their rarity, the length of the run (long runs have priority), and their condition.

CONCLUSION

Newspapers constitute a very valuable primary resource for scholarship in a number of fields, but they are difficult and expensive to acquire, house and process. They also present a huge preservation problem. Through the efforts of institutions such as CRL and programs such as the NEH U.S. Newspaper Program, progress in saving them is being made. A much larger effort must be made, however, if many existing files are to be kept from disappearing.

The Who, What, When, Where, Why and How of a Corporate Newspaper Library

Sandra E. Fitzgerald

SUMMARY. This article provides an overview of how one special library serves the information needs of a newspaper publisher. Policies and procedures are discussed, and overall conclusions are drawn.

Applied to today's newspaper reference library, the term "morgue" is a misnomer. Yesterday's term is not inclusive of today's activities. *Webster's New World Dictionary, Second College Edition,* defines morgue in the journalistic sense as the reference library of back numbers, photographs, clippings, etc., kept by a newspaper, magazine, etc., and hence a repository for material filed for possible future use. The term suggests storage of dead or little-used material. On the contrary, today's newspaper reference library is an evolving, energetic body striving to keep pace with the increasing demands of its corporate users, brought about by changing technology, as it operates within the framework of its individual parent organization.

When asked "Why does this library exist?" the seventeen staff members of the Indianapolis Newspapers Inc. Library responded with the following statements:

Sandra E. Fitzgerald is head librarian of the library that serves *The Indianapolis Star* and *The Indianapolis News*. Mailing address: Indianapolis Newspapers Inc., P.O. Box 145, Indianapolis, IN 46206-0145.

Author's Note: Upon accepting the invitation to write this article describing the work done in a library serving a newspaper staff, two thoughts were foremost in my mind. I realized that I was faced with the task of describing a multifaceted organization that exists to provide service by organizing materials, and that the Indianapolis Newspapers Inc. Library, serving two major daily newspapers, is comparable to many, but not all newspaper reference libraries. Although the services offered are similar to those of other newspaper reference libraries, the methods and procedures used in preparing the materials may differ.

- to serve the needs of the corporation . . . entailing a universal scope of information
- for public relations
- to support the aims, goals and objectives of both newspapers
- to provide service
- to document history for future use and maintain the quality of our newspapers
- to provide assistance to our subscribers and members of the general public
- to produce, maintain and make available factual information
- as a central location for the recording of history as it is created in Indianapolis
- to free newsroom staffers from maintaining time-consuming and redundant individual files
- to provide accurate and reliable information to reporters and the public as efficiently as possible

In summary, the priorities of the Indianapolis Newspapers Inc. Library, in this order, are to serve the newsrooms and other editorial departments of *The Indianapolis Star* and *The Indianapolis News*, as well as other in-house departments and the public on a limited basis. The library is charged with organizing materials to support these goals, while continuing to prove a cost-effective unit of the corporation. The library possesses the potential to generate future revenues.

Before addressing the "How is it done?" procedures, a few general comments must be made. The total number of the library staff is eighteen, six of whom are qualified to index the newspaper files and two of whom index the picture collection. All other staff are involved in reference, abstracting and other related clerical activities. The library serves patrons 18-1/2 hours daily, Monday through Saturday, and 13-1/2 hours on Sunday. There is one public service librarian who works exclusively with outside patrons. Additional public service is handled as staffing and in-house demands permit. All retention policies are based on in-house needs. The specific activities discussed in the remainder of this article are the development, control and maintenance of the clipping files, including microfilming procedures, picture and velox collection, books and periodicals, vertical file, electronic files, information retrieval services, reference services, including in-house and public service, and planning for an automated system.

CLIPPING FILE DEVELOPMENT, CONTROL AND MAINTENANCE

This section includes discussions of indexing in conjunction with the creation of an authority file and control, abstracting, filing of information, maintaining files and microfilming procedures.

Indexing

Articles selected from the final and early editions of both *The Star* and *The News* are indexed daily. Material retained from the final edition, or edition of record, is broad in scope, including state, local, national and international articles. Only state and local articles that did not appear in the final edition are retained from the early editions. All retention policies are based on in-house needs. Each daily publication is indexed by two librarians.

As a primary indexing tool, these librarians rely on the authority file, a product of an ongoing effort to control the creation of new file headings and to identify and revise outdated or misused terms. The indexers also use as guides the existing file, the *New York Times Index*, and *Sears List of Subject Headings*. Weekly indexing meetings are held. Following each meeting the head librarian and the librarian jointly responsible for subject heading control meet for discussion. As decisions are reached, authority cards are typed (see Example 1) and a memo is routed to the entire staff. The valid heading is entered into the clipping file, a hard copy authority file and an electronic file, which can be easily updated, printed out and distributed to the entire staff (see Example 2).

Using these tools, indexers assign appropriate file headings and cross references to the articles selected for retention. Subject file headings take the form of hierarchical breakdowns, a main heading coupled with one or more qualifiers. The indexer writes this information on the article and stamps each article with the name of the newspaper and the date of publication. Additional information includes page and column number and indexer identification. As each page is completed the indexer clips the articles from the newspaper for the abstractor.

Abstracting

The abstractor picks up material as it is completed by the indexer and scans the article to determine the file heading. This is the heading under which the clipping will be filed in an individual 4 inch by 6 inch envelope (see Example 3). The abstractor types the file heading on the

EXAMPLE 1. Authority File Cards.

```
                    Drivers Licenses


     See:   AUTOMOBILES--DRIVERS LICENSES
```

```
                        AUTOMOBILES--DRIVERS LICENSES


         x    Drivers Licenses
         x    Automobiles--Drivers--Licenses


    For material prior to 1974,
         See:   AUTOMOBILES--DRIVERS--LICENSES
```

Sandra E. Fitzgerald

EXAMPLE 2. Electronic Authority File Printout.

```
ID: INDEXV                                      DATE: 25-APR-86
NOTES: printout to library                      TIME: 14:37
DE:                                        RV: FITZ  :04/25,14:36


Van Accidents
Vandalism
Veterans
Veterans--Disabled
    See:  Veterans--Handicapped
Veterans--Handicapped
    x Veterans--Disabled
Victim Advocate Program Inc, Mar Co
    RT Crime, Task Force on Victims of
    RT Mar Co--Prosecutor--Victim/Witness Assistance Program
Video Recordings
    x Recordings--Video
    RT Tape Recordings
Violence--Domestic
    See:  Domestic Violence
Violence--Family
    See:  Domestic Violence
Volleyball
Volleyball--High School
Volunteers
Voters and Voting
Voters and Voting--Black
Voters and Voting--Youth
Voting Machines--Electronic
    x Voting Machines--Computerized
Voting Machines--Computerized
    See:  Voting Machines--Electronic
                            (END)
```

envelope, followed by a series of dashes which separates the heading from the body of the abstract. A concise abstract is prepared. The page and column number are indicated at the end of the abstract. The abstractor identification and a number indicating the day of the week are typed in the lower right corner.

The abstractor again scans the article to determine the cross reference headings. A cross reference heading and applicable abstract are typed at the top of a 4 inch by 6 inch card. A see-reference to the main envelope heading is typed at the bottom of the card, and the abstractor identification and day of the week are typed in the lower right corner. The envelopes and cards are then ready to be processed for filing.

Filing

As the abstracting process nears completion, a supervisor collects the material and stamps a publication date on each envelope and card. The material is checked for accuracy of indexing and abstracting quality, and is then alphabetized for filing. The current active file period is 1974 to the present. This means that clippings from *The Star* and *The News* for this period can be produced in original hard copy. Earlier clippings must be researched and copied from microfilm. Subject and

EXAMPLE 3. Abstracted Articles (Envelopes and Cards). THE STAR-Final edtn. THE NEWS-Early edtn.

```
Ind--Greenwood--Budget------------GRAFF ART/ The
                     proposed 1987 Greenwood city budget
   N AUG 1 1 1986    will be discussed tonight during
                     a public hearing held by the
Greenwood City Council.  Budget details are given.
21-1 METRO/J-S-H




SEE
   Ind--Greenwood--Council------------GRAFF ART/ The

                                                      w2
```

```
Graff, Jerry--Byline-------------The Greenwood City
                     Council will conduct a public hear-
   N AUG 1 1 1986    ing tonight to air their views on
                     the proposed city budget and
property tax rate.  The details of both issues are
given.  21-1 METRO/J-S-H




SEE
   Ind--Greenwood--Council------------GRAFF ART/ The

                                                      w2
```

EXAMPLE 3 (continued)

```
Ind--Greenwood--Council--------------GRAFF ART/ The
                        Greenwood City Council will con-
                        duct a public hearing tonight to
  N AUG 11 1986         air their views on the proposed
city budget and property tax rate.  The details of both
issues are given.  21-1 METRO/J-S-H




                                                      w2
```

```
Light, Betsy--Byline--------------PC/ Review of the new
                        Blake Edwards' movie, "A Fine Mess"
  S AUG 12 1986         starring Ted Danson and Howie
                        Mandel.   12-1




  SEE
Moving Pictures--A Fine Mess---------LIGHT ART/ Review
                                                      e3
```

EXAMPLE 3 (continued)

```
┌─────────────────────────────────────────────────────────────┐
│                                                             │
│  Moving Pictures--A Fine Mess----------LIGHT ART/ PC/       │
│                          Review of the new Blake Edwards'   │
│       S AUG 12 1986      movie starring Ted Danson and Howie│
│                          Mandel.  12-1                      │
│                                                             │
│                                                             │
│                                                             │
│                                                             │
│                                                       e3    │
│                                                             │
└─────────────────────────────────────────────────────────────┘


┌─────────────────────────────────────────────────────────────┐
│                                                             │
│  Taxes--Ind--Johnson County--Property----------GRAFF        │
│                          ART/ The 1987 property tax rate    │
│       N AUG 11 1986      for the city of Greenwood will be  │
│                          discussed tonight during a public  │
│  hearing held by the Greenwood City Council.  Details       │
│  of the issue are given.  21-1 METRO/J-S-H                  │
│                                                             │
│                                                             │
│                                                             │
│       SEE                                                   │
│     Ind--Greenwood--Council----------GRAFF ART/ The         │
│                                                             │
│                                                       w2    │
│                                                             │
└─────────────────────────────────────────────────────────────┘
```

biographical headings are interfiled, cards and envelopes appear in chronological order and are color-coded by year. Each file heading may include material from *The Star* and *The News*.

Special files are designated to accommodate certain fast-growing files, including those on the president of the United States, the Indiana governor, state senators and the Indianapolis mayor, as well as some ex-current and less frequently researched file. Pink envelopes are used for articles designated to remain permanently in the active file. The pink envelopes are not pulled for microfilming. The maintenance of clipping files includes shifting to accommodate growth areas, reading for filing errors, inserting file separators where needed and filing authority cards.

Microfilming

The active clipping files are weeded (material for specified years is pulled from the file) and microfilmed every three years. Currently all file entries dated 1974 through 1977 are being pulled for microfilming. Color-coding by year expedites the pulling of material. These files are edited by library staff members and sent to an outside firm to be processed. The films of file envelopes and cards, complete with abstracts, become a microfilm index that refers back to the complete issues of the newspapers on microfilm. A combined index for *The Star* and *The News* dates back to 1927. An index for *The News* only extends back to 1912.

PICTURE AND VELOX FILES

Three library staff members work in the picture area. One picture librarian is on duty in the evening hours. In addition to other responsibilities, two of these librarians index the picture collection. The scope of the picture and velox file is state, local, national and international.

All photographs, staff, wire and handout (both used and unused) come to the library for possible retention. These are stamped with an incoming date. All published photographs are separated into designated groups to be matched to a proof of publication cut from the newspaper. The indexer reviews both published and unpublished photographs for possible retention. If the photograph is to be retained, the indexer assigns a file heading and prints it in pencil on the back of the picture. If the photograph has been used, the proof of publication is taped to the back. A proof is affixed to the back of a photograph each time it is used. Photographs (both used and unused) not selected for retention are placed in the hold files, where they will be discarded after a specified period of time. Photographs to be retained are alphabetically sorted and filed in the permanent file.

Veloxes, made from the photographs and used in the printing process, are filed in the library. Only headshot veloxes of individuals are retained. Veloxes are filed separately from the picture collection.

Weeding of the picture and velox collection is ongoing. The library is not responsible for filing photo negatives.

BOOKS, PERIODICALS AND DAILY NEWSPAPER EDITIONS

The book collection, consisting of approximately 1300 volumes, is primarily a general reference collection. The collection is catalogued using the Dewey Decimal system. Books, with a few exceptions, may be signed out by newsroom personnel and other editorial department staff members. Books may not be kept out overnight without special permission.

Back issues of periodicals are retained for a six-month period. Periodicals may be signed out following book signout guidelines. Reading of the bookshelves is ongoing.

Complete issues of the final and state editions of *The Star* and *The News* are retained for 30 days for reference. These copies may not be cut or removed from the library, but are useful in finding articles not selected for retention.

VERTICAL FILES

The library maintains a vertical file housing supplemental materials not generated in-house. Biographical and subject files are maintained separately. One librarian is responsible for vertical file retention, indexing and reviewing existing files to discard materials. Preservation of vertical file materials is ongoing. Vertical file material can be signed out and returned at the end of the day. If necessary, materials may be retained by the user overnight.

ELECTRONIC FILES

While the electronically-maintained files are not accessed as frequently as the manually-maintained clipping files, they serve a significant purpose. These files are an educational resource as well as a valuable reference tool.

The electronic files are being created in the Atex editorial front-end system, and offer librarians and newsroom staff the opportunity to become familiar with the processing and searching of information electronically. Becoming familiar with the front-end system is a logical step for librarians in laying the groundwork for an automated library system. This will be discussed in more detail in a later section on planning for an automated system.

Files are created as the reporters' needs occur. Examples of such files might include: lists of personal names and titles, university faculty, public officials and community organizations; chronologies on heart transplants, hostage situations and police shootings; and unpublished articles pulled from the newsroom wire queues (see Example 4). The library is also developing files for the Pan-American Games, which are to be held in Indianapolis in 1987.

There are five queues in the library system. The library-created information files are stored in three separate queues. One queue is available to *The Star*, one to *The News*, and one can be accessed by both newspapers. This protects confidential material for each newspaper. Information files are processed in another queue available only to the library staff. Another queue is available only to the head librarian. Here departmental information is processed and stored. As mentioned earlier, the library is building a subject authority file in the Atex system. This file is stored in the head librarian's queue. Printouts are updated as necessary for library staff members.

INFORMATION RETRIEVAL SERVICES

To keep pace with changing technology and the broadening scope of newspapers, the library will be offering online information retrieval services to the reporting staff. As with all new services, the groundwork was laid carefully. The need was identified, and a committee of newsroom staff, library personnel and systems technicians selected the appropriate hardware, software and information services. Access to Dialog, Nexis and Dow Jones is planned, and training sessions will prepare library staff to use these services. The new arrangement will be evaluated and changes implemented to meet the reporters' needs.

REFERENCE SERVICES

It has been stated that a newspaper reference library exists to provide service by organizing materials. Hence, the reason the materials are being organized must be kept in mind at all times. Systems should be designed to meet the information demands within the framework of

EXAMPLE 4. Electronic Reference File; Printout of One Page.

```
ID: INDHEARTS                                          DATE: 13-AUG-86
NOTES: Indpls Heart Transplants                        TIME: 08:05
DE:                                              RV: FITZ  ;08/13;08:03


        The following is a list of 29 of the 37 persons receiving heart
transplants at Methodist Hospital & information regarding each case, where
available. The cases appear in the order the transplants occurred.
        Methodist Hospital disclosed plans June 26 to begin performing artificial
heart transplants as a bridge to keep patients alive until a human heart
becomes available. It is hoped such surgery could take place by early 1987.
        Also included is a list of the transplants done at the Indiana
University Medical Center, the first of which occured June 1, 1986.

SOURCE:   INDPLS STAR & NEWS LIBRARY FILES AND THE WIRE SERVICES

METHODIST HOSPITAL TRANSPLANTS

    1.  ANNA GARDNER
        Age: 39
        Crawfordsville
        Housewife
        Underwent Surgery:  October 30, 1982
        Disease: Congenital Deterioration of Heart Muscle
        Surgeon:  Dr. Harold G. Halbrook, Indpls
        Released:  January 7, 1983

    2.  JOHN R. MCNEELY
        Age: 52
        950 Garfield Drive East, Indpls
        Retired fire fighter
        Underwent Surgery:  February 4, 1983
        Disease: Cardiac Disease, Heart attack suffered May 1982
        Surgeon:  Dr. Harold G. Halbrook
        Released:  March 23, 1983
        Died January 29, 1984, Kidney failure & Pneumonia

    3.  DENNIS LEE MAST
        Age: 18
        Napanee
        Underwent Surgery:  June 3, 1983
        Disease: Familial Cardiomyopathy (progressive deterioration of heart
                 muscle
        Surgeon:  Dr. Harold G. Halbrook
        Released:  July 21, 1983
        Died January 15, 1986, irregularity and rejection of the heart.

    4.  JOHN A. SCHWEIR
        Age:  50
        Chesterton
        Pharmacist
        Underwent Surgery:  June 27, 1983
        Disease: Coronary artery disease, Heart attacks June 1981 & April 1982
        Surgeon:  Dr. Harold G. Halbrook
        Donor:  Michael R. Newhouse, 30, Indpls, victim of motorcycle accident
        Died:  August 23, 1983, Heart attack
                            (MORE)
```

corporate structure and available time. "How do we do it?" must not be permitted to overshadow "Why do we do it?"

The organizational structure (the development and maintenance of materials) of the Indianapolis Newspapers Inc. Library has already been discussed in some detail. This section will look at how these library resources are accessed by both in-house users and the public.

Services offered to primary users, the reporting staffs of *The Star* and *The News*, will be examined first.

Reporters and editors may telephone or come to the library for information. Only library personnel have access to clipping reference files, the photograph and velox collection and the vertical file. Reporters and editors coming to the library for information must request assistance in these areas. Although newsroom staff may not retrieve, refile or remove original clippings from the library, policies are flexible enough to meet individual needs. A specific article or fact can be requested, and a library staff member will research, copy, and send the results to the user. Reporters may request an entire file from which they can personally select any number of articles. All selected clipping material is copied. Reference requests are completed on a priority basis, as newsroom deadlines dictate.

A request can be as simple as verifying the full name and party affiliation of an Indiana senator. On the other hand, it can be as difficult as a request once received to locate articles involving a specific homicide. The only information given to the librarian was that the incident had occurred somewhere in Indiana and that the body was found in a field with the victim's clothing in a neat pile nearby. The articles were found!

The reporting staff may access the book card catalog and browse the bookshelves and periodical shelves, but these materials must be signed out by a librarian before being removed from the library. Reporters are encouraged to access the electronic files from their desks, whenever possible. The library also provides copies of articles and series for entry in writing contests sponsored by professional and community organizations such as the Hoosier State Press Association, the Indiana Associated Press Managing Editors and the Community Service Council of Metropolitan Indianapolis.

In addition to the services provided to newsroom staff, the library receives requests from other departments within the company, such as advertising, circulation and public relations. Recently the library assisted in the selection and reproduction of page prints to be used in the creation of an umbrella for a circulation promotion.

The public service librarian's hours are 8 A.M. to 5 P.M., Monday through Friday. She assists outside patrons with clipping reference at the counter, by telephone and by mail. Service to the public is provided on a limited basis, as written policy dictates. Generally, public service is limited to requests that can be dealt with quickly in consulting the newspaper files. An index (copies of envelope and card file entries) can be provided for the active file period (see Example 5).

EXAMPLE 5. Index. (Record of File Entries.) This Sample Includes Cards and Envelopes for All 1986 Articles in A. J. Foyt File.

```
Foyt, A J-------------BENNER B ART/ PC/ A J Foyt, the
                      only four-time winner of the Indpls
  S MAY 1 2 1986      500, yesterday qualified for his
                      29th consecutive race with an
average of 213.212 mph. This made him the fifth fast-
est qualifier. DETAILS  13-4




       SEE
Automobile Races--Indpls 500--Qualifications------------
              BENNER B ART/
                                                     g2
```

```
Foyt, A J-------------CADOU ART/ SPORTS ON THE AIR/
                      Foyt is the owner of Rare Brick,
  S MAR 2 9 1986      the only unbeaten 3 year old in
                      training for the Triple Crown horse-
racing events. DETAILS  31-1




       SEE
Cadou, Jep Jr--Byline--------------SPORTS
                                                     y7
```

EXAMPLE 5 (continued)

Foyt, A J----------DENNY & MITTMAN ART/ PC/ A J Foyt
                   represents some of the very
N MAY 19 1986 experienced drivers to be found in
                   this year's Indpls 500. 17-1

Automobile Races--Indpls 500--Qualifications-----------
                   DENNY
                                                      h2

Foyt, A J---------------DUNKIN ART/ PC/ If Foyt is
                        supposed to win the Indpls 500 in
N MAY 12 1986   10-year intervals, his next win
                        shouldn't come until next year,
but he says he feels really good this year. 21-1

SEE

Automobile Races--Indpls 500--Qualifications-----------
                   PC/
                                                      h2

EXAMPLE 5 (continued)

```
Foyt, A J---------------Four-time Indpls 500 Mile Race
                        winner entered five cars into the
                        1986 Indpls 500 yesterday increas-
   S FEB 16 1986        ing the official entry list to
                        26.  11-4-B












   SEE
   Automobile Races--Indpls 500--Entries----------------
          A J Foyt
                                                      a1
```

```
Foyt, A J---------------Foyt has driven in more Indpls
                        500 races than any other driver,
   N FEB 17 1986        and has entered 5 cars for the
                        500 this year.  He hopes for a
spot in the starting lineup for a record 29th consecu-
tive year.  20-1










   SEE
   Automobile Races--Indpls 500--Entries----------------
          A J Foyt
                                                      s2
```

EXAMPLE 5 (continued)

```
Foyt, A J--------------FUSON ART/ GASOLINE ALLEY/ A J
                       Foyt, the only four-time winner
   N MAY 23 1986       of the Indpls 500 Mile Race, knows
                       all about what it takes to win.
                       16-1




  SEE
  Fuson, Wayne--Byline------------GASOLINE

                                                       m6
```

```
Foyt, A J--------------GARLICK ART/ PC/ A technical
                       problem cost A J Foyt a shot at
   S MAY 11 1986       qualifying for the Indpls 500
                       yesterday.  8-5-D




  SEE
  Automobile Races--Indpls 500--Qualifications----------
                     WALTERS
                                                       h1
```

EXAMPLE 5 (continued)

```
Foyt, A J--------------MITTMAN ART/ AUTO RACING/
                       According to Al Bloemker, vice
   N MAR 7 - 1986      president of the Indpls Motor
                       Speedway, neither A J Foyt nor
anyone else was ever given appearance money to compete
in the Indpls 500.  Foyt claimed that he had received
money from every track where he has raced.   17-1




SEE
Mittman, Dick--Byline--------------AUTO RACING/

                                                    m6
```

```
Foyt, A J-------------MITTMAN ART/ Foyt did some of
                      his best racing in years yesterday
   N FEB 1 7 1986     in the Daytona 500, but his car
                      engine still wouldn't get him to
the finish line.   16-5




SEE
Automobile Races--Florida-----------MITTMAN ART/

                                                    m2
```

EXAMPLE 5 (continued)

```
Foyt, A J--------------MITTMAN ART/ PC/ At the age of
                      51, A J Foyt is ready to attack
  N MAY 8 - 1986  the Indpls 500 again.  Foyt has
                   had only one top 10 finish in the
last seven Indpls 500s.  He started 24th, 12th and
21st in the last three.  DETAILS  34-5




SEE
Automobile Races--Indpls 500-------------MITTMAN ART/
                                                    q5
```

```
Foyt, A J-------------This four-time winner of the
                      Indpls 500 Mile Race is the mile-
  N MAY 1 9 1986      age leader in racing career of all
                      drivers in the 70th Indpls 500
to be run on May 25.  DETAILS  21-1




                                                    a2
```

Outside patrons are allowed to research the microfilm index. Private fee-based research is offered for in-depth requests.

In-house requests for photographs and veloxes are handled by picture department staff members. Newsroom staff and other company personnel may browse through picture folders after they have been pulled from the file by a library staff member. Requests for photographs to be reprinted in other publications or to be used for commercial purposes are referred to the library picture department. A picture librarian obtains the required approval and processes the request.

PLANNING FOR AN AUTOMATED SYSTEM

A computerized retrieval system is still a few years away at the Indianapolis Newspaper Inc. Library, but steps have already been taken toward that eventuality. Early planning and preparation is vital to maintaining library credibility, while continuing to meet the information demands of the users. The first logical step is the gathering of information. This will assist in identifying concerns and avoiding many pitfalls. Some ways of gathering this information can include:

- attending professional workshops and conventions
- reading the literature
- becoming familiar with computer terminology
- visiting libraries where systems are being and have been implemented

It is recognized that time must be allowed in the planning stage to develop a general awareness of the broad picture. The following is a list of questions to be considered, as groundwork is being laid for system development:

- How will the library system interface with the editorial system?
- What can the editorial front-end system contribute?
- What must the system do?
- How will the staff be trained?
- How will newsroom staff be trained?
- How will library material be processed?
- Will system products be marketed to outsiders to offset cost?

As discussed earlier, one of the initial steps in preparing for library automation was gaining an understanding of the editorial front-end system. The head librarian took the training classes offered by Atex, when this system was brought into the newsrooms. This hands-on introduction to the handling of information electronically was worthwhile in that understanding the newsroom system can save the library time when it designs its own system.

The library has acquired an Atex terminal and is beginning to set up the files needed to provide service to the newsrooms and to educate librarians and newsroom staff in the development and use of electronic information files. With the new terminal's offering access to information retrieval systems, another interim step has been taken in the direction of complete library automation.

The recommendation has been made to management that when a definite goal is set for library automation, a committee be formed consisting of library personnel, newsroom staff and in-house systems technicians to select and implement the system.

CONCLUSION

In this article, the approach one special library takes in serving the information needs of its parent organization has been discussed. An attempt has been made to reveal a dynamic, vital and complex organization constantly moving forward with changing technology. Such an organization must remain flexible and sensitive to the needs of its users, and most importantly, it must outgrow the label "morgue."

Education for Newspaper Librarianship

Mary Ellen Soper

SUMMARY. This paper offers a discussion of whether there is need for library schools to provide special preparation for newspaper librarianship. In the author's opinion, such training is probably not a high priority, and is unlikely to become a separate part of the curriculum. It is postulated that short courses and workshops should take care of any such need.

It is unlikely that an accredited library school would have a course devoted exclusively to newspaper librarianship as part of its regular curriculum, though it could occasionally offer workshops or short courses on the subject. Most accredited schools offer one-year programs in which they prepare students to be professional librarians, with a master's degree. In such programs there is insufficient time to offer many courses designed to prepare people for narrow, specialized positions in libraries and information centers. Attempts are made to prepare for broader functions, such as cataloging, reference work, administration, children's services, management of automated systems, etc. Instructors can also try to introduce students to the features specific to various types of libraries, such as academic and research, public, school, and special libraries.

Attempts may also be made to introduce students to special types of materials, such as government publications (assumed special because in many libraries they have often been excluded from the type of treatment given to print materials), children's and young adults' materials (assumed special because of the maturation levels of the intended users), and materials published serially (assumed special because they continue to arrive, a condition that can result in significant changes among the various parts of an item). An interesting side-effect of of-

---

Mary Ellen Soper, Assistant Professor, Graduate School of Library and Information Science, University of Washington.

fering courses devoted to the acquisition, organization, and use of specific types of materials is the need to emphasize definitions; there is great overlap between the types of materials and the intended users in each category. For example: government publications, that can be in print or audio-visual formats, are intended for a wide variety of ages and educational levels in the population, and are both monographically and serially published. Even definitions based on the source, when used for government publications, are fraught with all sorts of interesting problems.

If a special course could be devoted just to the management and use of newspapers, it would first be necessary to define and set limits on what is meant by the term "newspaper." The definition in the *ALA Glossary of Library and Information Science* is not very limiting: "A serial issued at stated, frequent intervals (usually daily, weekly, or semiweekly), containing news, opinion, advertisements, and other items of current, often local, interest."[1] The most useful part of this definition would seem to be the last part, which is concerned with the intended use. But where in this case do such "national" newspapers as the *New York Times, USA Today, Wall Street Journal*, and the *Christian Science Monitor* fit? The frequency is not very helpful; newsletters and other serials could be daily, while many other serials are weekly or semiweekly. The mentioned contents can appear in many types of serial publications. "Currency" appears to be the important element: newspapers are designed to supply current, ever changing news, and they are issued as frequently as possible, on inexpensive papers so that the cost is kept as low as practicable in order to reach a wide audience. Currency, however, is also an important feature of radio and television news and opinion, so currency alone is not sufficient to set a limit on what newspapers are and are not.

Even the type of paper characteristically used for newspapers is not a particularly good limiting factor anymore. Most newspapers that libraries intend to preserve are filmed and kept in a microformat because the original paper is rarely designed for longevity. The filmed contents are, however, still considered to be newspapers. Contents of some newspapers are now also available in machine-readable form, and can be accessed easily on various automated systems. Yet they are still identified as newspapers in spite of the altered format.

Once it is decided what is meant by newspapers, an attempt can then be made to determine what should be included in a course on

---

[1]*ALA Glossary of Library and Information Science*. Heartsill Young, editor. Chicago: American Library Association, 1983: p. 153.

newspaper librarianship. A brief history of newspapers and an overview of their importance in our lives could be presented first. Collection development/management would probably occupy a segment, since newspapers tend to be expensive purchases and require special storage and preservation facilities. What titles to acquire and how long to keep them is determined by the library's publics and by budgetary factors. As these also determine what other types of materials, in what quantities, a library will have in its collections, newspapers cannot be considered unique, except perhaps in the rather high encumbrance each newspaper title entails.

Acquisition of newspapers would not require any special training, other than that needed for any type of material in pointing out the particular reference tools that have to be consulted. If newspapers are to be kept for only a short time, cataloging should involve little more than listing the city, title, frequency, period of retention, and where the title is located in the library. If the title is to be kept in the permanent collection then the cataloging becomes more complicated, because newspapers are notorious for changeable titles, and can be susceptible to erratic frequencies. Newspapers are nonetheless serials; if a good foundation is provided in serials cataloging, there is little need to add anything more to cover newspapers.* Attention to problems of headings for geographic names is necessary, but this is also required for other materials.

Special display and storage facilities are needed for newspapers, but since these are obvious, discussion here is really unnecessary. Preservation certainly needs to be considered; newspapers have been recognized as particular problems in this area for many years, and much of the microfilming done in libraries has been of newspapers. The elements that have to be covered in preservation microfilming are not, however, unique to newspapers: checking that the item to be filmed is complete; using a standard reduction ratio, being careful to produce legible frames; using film stock that is safe and durable; processing the exposed film correctly; using archival storage containers, etc.**

It is on the area of use that the greatest stress could be placed. The key to successful utilization of newspapers lies in indexing the contents. Indexing newspapers is analogous to indexing journals and books; provision is made to access the microlevel, or contents, of the

---

*Editor's Note: For further discussion of this topic, see Upham's article in this volume and the Summer 1986 issue of *Cataloging & Classification Quarterly*.

**Editor's Note: For more information about preservation, see Miller's article on microfilming and Lund's on preservation, both found elsewhere in this volume.

item, and not just the macrolevel, or the whole. Newspaper indexing has had to be done by many libraries in the past, since there is a demand for such access. (When the author first went to library school, students were told they could use the *New York Times* printed index to find dates in order to avoid having to do their own indexing of local papers. Obviously, if there is much interest in events on the local level, this is not sufficient. Even national and international events might have a local twist that national newspaper indexes miss.)*

The principles and techniques of indexing are the same for all types of material, although newspapers require some special considerations. As the names of people, places, and events make up an important part of newspaper contents, and are also frequently sought by users, stress must be placed on how to handle proper names and their variant forms. Decisions have to be made as to how much of a newspaper should be indexed. Should the following be included: the classified ads; sports sections; births, deaths and wedding announcements; the activities of local organizations such as theatre and music groups; movie listings, etc.? Local newspapers are often of great interest to historians and genealogists, and so it may be necessary to index these in greater depth than is done for journals or monographic publications. The extent of indexing done should be based on users' known and potential needs; in reality it is likely to be determined by economic considerations. But it should be kept in mind that stinting on indexing to save the library money will likely result in costing the user much more in time, effort, and inability to locate information than the library saves.

Since some newspapers are available in automated databases, attention should be paid to how these databases are accessed, and how they can be efficiently and profitably searched. But after the unique characteristics of the newspaper files are made known, the principles of online searching apply in this case as in that of all other automated data files.

CONCLUSION

Because library schools presently teach such subjects as collection development/management, cataloging, reference service, online searching, preservation and indexing, there is little apparent need for a

---

*****Editor's Note**: For further information about newspaper indexing, see Starkey's article elsewhere in this volume.

separate, regular course in newspaper librarianship. What could be usefully offered would be a short course, workshop or institute on the elements of the subject that are considered unique to newspaper organization in libraries and to libraries in newspaper offices. Such offerings might include information on the history of newspapers, their importance in libraries, how to index and access them effectively, and the special aspects of preserving them for the future. Another element that might be covered is the need for union listing of newspapers so that the rich variety of titles held by libraries is known to potential users. As most libraries can acquire a few newspapers and preserve these few for continued use, such materials are in particular need of being shared in order to enhance the store of information available to the library public. If the emphasis is to be on libraries in newspaper organizations, then the handling of clipping files might need to be covered.

In the 1985-86 issue of the Association for Library and Information Science Education directory, there is no classification for newspapers under special materials. It cannot, therefore, be determined if any accredited schools do offer regular newspaper librarianship courses. The chances are that there are few or none. Nor apparently is there an ALA standing committee that is primarily concerned with newspapers, although the Special Libraries Association has had a Newspaper Division since 1924. In the 1985-86 SLA directory, the Division was shown to have 467 members, and the officers were all employed in libraries operated by newspapers. SLA appears to be the obvious organization in which newspaper librarians can be expected to participate. *Library Literature* lists a scattering of articles under the heading: NEWSPAPER LIBRARIES and NEWSPAPERS. These may be useful for finding help in solving problems and in obtaining ideas for planning.

Most newspaper librarians probably learn on the job. This is not likely to be reassuring to library school students, since they do not always realize they are learning the principles and techniques they will need in the other courses they are taking in the curriculum. There does not appear to be much possibility that formal library school education will be provided specifically for newspaper librarianship in the near future; and unless it can be shown that the present situation in our graduate education is really unsatisfactory and in need of major changes, there probably will not be.

There's Gold in Them Thar Reels: Or How Microfilmed Newspapers Saved a Region's History

Charles L. Sullivan

SUMMARY. This article, written from the personal perspective of the author, chronicles some of the discoveries he made with regard to the richness and color of the newspaper articles used during the writing of his two recent books. Liberal quotations are included as examples of the style and content of columns discovered in a number of Gulf Coast newspapers.

"This is God's judgment. It is a token of His wrath and displeasure; for the people here drink too much whisky, play cards too much, and never look out for but themselves," so remonstrated a well known, well off and very religious resident of Pascagoula, Mississippi, at the height of the hurricane of September 14, 1860. Soon after his outburst of piety "the gentleman gathered up several boxes of claret and a whole lot of sardines, which had been washed away from the wreck of the little coffee house by the wharf, and stored them away in a back room of his house for his own future use."

The foregoing report, contained on page one of the *New Orleans Daily Cresent* for September 19, 1860, further stated the name of the

---

Charles L. Sullivan is the Chairman of the Social Studies Department at the Perkinston Campus of the Mississippi Gulf Coast Junior College. He holds a master's degree from the University of Southern Mississippi and has completed PhD coursework at the University of Mississippi. He is the author of *The Mississippi Gulf Coast: Portrait of a People* and *Hurricanes of the Mississippi Gulf Coast*.

Editor's Note: This paper was solicited as a personal account by the author of discoveries made while doing research for two books on the Mississippi Gulf Coast.

holier than thou thief (Baptiste), the name of the owner of the stolen goods (Antoine) and offered "the name of our informant on this point . . . to . . . anyone who may want it." The full article, which when transcribed runs to three and one half pages of single spaced type, includes also the selfless heroism of Jules Feret, a young New Orleanian, who repeatedly risked his life to save others from storm-surge splintered houses. Those of us on the Mississippi Gulf Coast today would know nothing of the heroes and villains of 1860 if information about them had not been saved in the newspaper files of New Orleans.

As a doctoral student at the University of Mississippi I studiously avoided newspapers as a source when I wrote term papers. In the first place, I did not have a very high regard for the accuracy of newspapers. In the second place, the dizzying and time-consuming search through spinning reels of microfilm in quest of uncertain reward was not to my liking. In the third place, I do not care for modern "newspaperese," in which the malefactor "allegedly" did the deed and wherein "an unnamed source close to the top" leaked this or that information. I understand that modern newspapers must bow to 20th century libel and slander laws. On the other hand, wading through a swamp of ambiguous phraseology is not my idea of a good time.

Nineteenth century newspapermen, however, played by different rules (if any existed), and they played hardball, as evidenced in the report on the hurricane of 1860 given above. Furthermore, 19th century libel cases were settled at 20 paces under the oaks. The *New Orleans Daily Delta* for July 26, 1856, carried an announcement that illuminates that aspect of Victorian Age journalism:

> We have the pleasure of announcing to the readers of the (Yazoo City, Mississippi) *American Banner* that Mr. John T. Smith, an able writer and a zealous American, who has been connected with the Mississippi Press for fourteen years, has been engaged to take charge of the Political Department of the paper . . .
>
> Mr. Smith, though a remarkably courteous and amiable gentleman, has fought five duels, killing his man every time.
>
> He brings . . . besides, a general stock of political information and zeal for the cause, two Bowie knives, one of Parson Beecher's rifles, two six-shooters, and sundry canes and shillelahs, not to speak of two pairs of brass knuckles.
>
> P. S. Challenges received from 9 o'clock to 3 p.m.

During the June, 1868, elections for the Mississippi State legislature, Pizzaro K. Mayers, ex-Confederate officer and editor of the *Handsboro Democrat* published a piece in which he branded Benjamin Orr, Radical Republican scalawag and candidate for office, as a "liar, a scoundrel and a thief." On July 8th the unsuccessful office seeker and his son Henry went eyeball to eyeball at "high noon" with P. K. on the main street of Pass Christian. Benjamin drew, P. K. blew him away with a charge of buckshot, and then swiveled the shotgun on Henry. Alas, the gun misfired. Henry shot the editor in the wrist, but his other five bullets harmlessly shattered store windows as Mayers raced to safety along the board sidewalk.

The Southern newspaperman of the past century backed up his pen with the sword, and that is precisely why the newspapers of the era are so valuable to modern research historians. Furthermore, many of the articles are minor literary masterpieces packed with a wealth of detail, often humorous and written with a clarity and precision not often seen today.

This from the *New Orleans Daily Cresent* for August 13, 1860, regarding a problem inherent in the feminine attire of the time:

The stiff gusts sent many a hat and umbrella kiting; sheds and fences got the rickets, and some flopped over; and this important fact has known numerous instances—that ladies who *will* wear hoops and *will* expose themselves to the vagaries of a high wind, should be prepared for disaster, and wear some part of their raiment, or more thereof than usual, inside their hoops. We heard of several pitiable spectacles of ladies outraged by the wind on the public streets.

Those who think that yellow journalism was a post-Civil War phenomenon are in for a surprise. In the ante-bellum period, the steamboats offered the only connection between the towns of the Mississippi Gulf Coast and the flanking cities of New Orleans and Mobile. The hurricane of 1860 stranded hundreds of vacationing New Orleanians in Biloxi. When the steamboat *Alabama* arrived there two days late, bound the wrong way, and carrying no food or ice, the crowd coalesced into a mob and turned nasty. The *New Orleans Daily Cresent* got wind of the ruckus and the headlines for September 21, 1860, made William Randolph Hearst's later stuff look like a third grade fistfight on the playground.

> INTERESTING NEWS
> FROM BILOXI AND THE GULF SHORE
> ANOTHER OUTRAGE BY THE MONOPOLY
> THE STEAMER *ALABAMA* MOBBED
> DISTRESS AND EXCITEMENT ALONG THE COAST
> PROTEST OF THE MAIL LINE
> THEIR SIDE OF THE AFFAIR
> NO BOAT TO TOUCH AT BILOXI
> THE PEOPLE THERE TO GET HOME AS BEST THEY CAN
> GREAT EXCITEMENT

On the next day the headlines read:

> THE MAIL LINE OUTRAGE
> THE BLOCKAGE OF BILOXI
> THE DISTRESS OF CITY FAMILIES OVER THERE
> ARRIVAL OF ANOTHER SCHOONER LOAD OF SUFFERERS
> EXCITEMENT UNABATED

Also on page one the editor stated and not as an "editorial":

> We are of opinion that Company has perpetrated the most inexcusable, unmitigated, and dastardly outrage that ever any company inflicted upon white people during the whole history of steamboating.
> Our limits forbid our giving some other things that we would like to state in this connection.

It makes one wonder what the limits were. What there is would peel the chrome off a bumper.

Another thing not commonly known about the journalism of the last century, most likely a product of the modern misconception of the Victorian Age, is how risqué it could be. Before reading further, be reminded that the fountain of youth sought by Ponce de León was a fabled spring noted for its aphrodisiacal qualities. The following comes from the *New Orleans Daily Delta*, September 8, 1853, regarding a visit to Ocean Springs, Mississippi:

> I find myself anchored at this charming resort, under the impression that the fabled waters sought for with so much diligence by Ponce de León could have been found by that very respectable old codger if he had jumped on board the first skiff in readiness and embarked for Ocean Springs.
> I find James A. Valentine . . . rejuvenated and refreshed by his stay here . . . he is appropriately, in his own language, "The delight of daughters, and fear of mothers."

Apparently when not imbibing love potions, the people of the time played the "Peeping Tom" or went skinny-dipping. This from Mississippi City as quoted in the "New Orleans Daily Delta" September 17, 1851. The "meek little domicile," incidentally, is a bathing box or bath house. Such were a feature of coastal life until the early years of this century. Attached to the wharves, some were for the use of men and others for the fairer sex:

> Now prithee, good friend, avert your gaze from that meek little domicile that rears its modest proportions beside this self same wharf. Within its depths, I hear the smothered splashing of waters, and I think I detect the merry laugh of joyous maids.
> I ask you to bend your vision otherways, for there are wide interstices between the posts that support that meek tenement, and, mayhap, an enterprising look will disclose a nude limb or the gourgeous swell of an unruffled bust. In some case fierce calamity may overtake you. Mythological records tell us that to gaze upon an unclothed goddess was death to curious mortals, and in my mad devotion to the female sex, I style them all *divine*.
> In earlier days, ere my hair was whitened by the paint of Time, I loved a gleesome girl, and from her young and immaculate heart surged forth a wild torrent of reciprocating affection. I was at her father's house. She was a rustic beauty, with small feet, for the soil was poor. Very early in the morning I passed the apartment that contained the object of my fierce attachment. The heedless creature had permitted the door to remain unclosed.
> I saw—no matter what I saw. A terrific scream resounded through the house, and in a few moments I received an unperfumed billet from dear girl, requesting my immediate departure. The note said in conclusion: "A man what is a man, has no business to look at a female anyhow until she is dressed up."
> Hence my bachelorhood—hence do I warn you, good friend,

to avert your gaze from that bathing house replete with laughing nudities.

But, come on with me. There's rare fun in reserve for us. We are now sufficiently removed from mortal vision. Let us tear from our persons all evidence of the first great transgressions; for I do hold that had not Adam addicted himself to fruit, the pettycoat and pantaloon would have been the topics of a crazy poet's dream, and not tasteless and concealing articles of attire!

They did not mince words either, and they could be very raunchy. This from Ocean Springs quoted from the *New Orleans Daily Delta*, July 22, 1856:

One Susan Cassidy, a notorious drunkard, was found in a ditch, in a dying condition, and with one or two slight scratches and contusions on her person. She died, and her husband was arrested on suspicion.

Both the woman and her husband were proved to have been habitual drunkards, and some curious definitions of drunkenness were given . . . [at the trial].

Benjamin Williams, witness, said: I do not consider a man *very* drunk until he has to lie down; I never think myself drunk till I can't walk; Cassidy was not able to stand or walk when I left him; I can drink about a gallon of whisky a day, a quart is not anything.

H. F. Williams—chip of the old block, I suppose—swore; Cassidy left my grocery *half snapped*; half snapped means half drunk; I consider a man *whole snapped* when he falls over and tumbles every time he tries to get up; when he can't come the perpinduclars, but sort o' horizontalizes, he is dead up, or clean gone; I have often seen the prisoner in this fix, and his wife half seas over.

The verdict: Mr. Cassidy innocent by reasons of being *whole snapped* and thus in no condition to murder Mrs. Cassidy, who therefore must have died accidentally.

Another thing that may not be generally known is that 19th century newspapers quoted one another sometimes with marvelous results. To my knowledge no scrap of original antebellum newspaper exists on the coast other than a torn fragment of one printed in 1855. However, the first two issues of the first newspaper ever printed in Ocean Springs exist reprinted verbatim in the microfilm of the *New Orleans Daily Picayune*. Vol. 1, Number 1, of the *Ocean Springs Naiad* is contained in the *Daily Picayune* of September 14, 1853 and the Vol. 1, Number 2, *Naiad* of September 18 appeared in the *Daily Picayune* of September 21st. I do not know of another such instance, but think it worthwhile for small towns seeking their lost newspapers to check the files of long-running newspapers in nearby cities.

The reprinting of a whole issue of a newspaper inside another may not have been unique, as articles reprinted in this way were quoted often. For example, the *New Orleans Daily Delta* of July 22, 1851, extracted from the *Biloxi Seashore Sentinel* of July 15 this murder story:

> We learn from the *Seashore Sentinel* that a most shocking murder was committed at Biloxi on Tuesday evening last (July 15, 1851).
>
> A man named Bartolo San Andro had quarreled with an Italian named Bernardo about three weeks before. On Tuesday evening they met not far from the Magnolia Hotel, when the latter stabbed the former in his back and side with a sword cane, producing almost immediate death.
>
> The murderer was at the time pursued, but escaped. He was afterwards arrested through the agency of the Mate of the steamboat *California*, which boat he got on board of at Mississippi City.
>
> Bernardo has been examined om the charge and held to bail in the sum of $2,000 — a small sum, under the circumstances.
>
> He had with him a sword-cane which corresponded exactly with the wounds of the murdered man and his conduct was every way suspicious.

From this jewel of Biloxiana, which exists in no other form, we learn of one ethnic group, the major mode of travel, bail-bond amounts, and in particular a bit of antebellum forensic science. I mean — the police must have stuck the sword in the corpse's wounds if the last sentence of the story is truly accurate.

Dealing with newspapers, has altered my perception of the 19th century, a change that came about quite accidentally. The Mississippi Coast and Genealogical Society asked me to write a book entitled *Mississippi Gulf Coast: Portrait of a People*. I told them I would do it, if I could find enough primary sources from which to extract an historically true picture of what had happened. Those witches and warlocks (i.e., hurricanes) from the gulf which have pounded this area from time immemorial have seen to it that few structures from bygone eras exist here, much less written records and photographs. A journey to the Mississippi State Department of Archives and History revealed very little material bearing directly on the southern area of the state. There are several reasons for that, not the least being that no direct communication lines existed between the Mississippi Gulf Coast and the capital until very recent times.

The history of the six counties that form the panhandle of southernmost Mississippi (bounded on the north by the 31st parallel, on the south by the barrier islands of the Gulf, on the west by the Pearl River and on the east by the Pascagoula River) has always turned on an east-west axis anchored in the flanking cities of New Orleans and Mobile. Luckily for me someone else had already figured that out. M. James Stevens came from New Jersey to the Mississippi Gulf Coast 40 years ago. As the proprietor of the Confederate Inn in Biloxi, he developed a keen interest in the history of the area and asked a lot of questions that no one could answer. The search for answers led him into the newspaper files of New Orleans and Mobile, and that is where he struck the mother lode—literally.

In the antebellum period six towns grew along the Mississippi Coast between New Orleans and Mobile. Termed the Six Sisters because they were "daughters" of the two flanking cities, these were Shieldsboro (now Bay St. Louis), Pass Christian, Mississippi City-Handsboro, Biloxi, Ocean Springs and Pascagoula. The Six Sisters served the metropolitan areas on either side via steamboat as a playground and as a refuge from summer heat and the threat of yellow fever. Many of the inhabitants of the two cities held dual citizenship and spent the summer or even a greater part of the year on the coast. Hence, both cities evinced an avid interest in doings in the Six Sisters. Every major newspaper had one or more correspondents in each coast town and regularly published their letters. These missives were not "letters to the editor" but whole slices of life from a particular place at a particular time. The correspondents were apparently very well-educated individuals who wrote under pseudonyms such as Gdoubleyou, Patriarch Dismal, Snap Beans, and Bill Peas (who in one letter signed himself as "no relation to Snap Beans").

Stevens has spent several decades of his life hunting those letters on microfilm. A New Jersey state champion typist he typed them up and placed them in chronological order in large loose leaf binders. At present he has amassed in this manner approximately 53,000 total documents.

When Stevens heard that I was to write the book and could find precious few sources, he made his massive collection available to me, thus afflicting this writer with an uncommon malady—too much magnificent eyewitness material to use. In three years I read most of his collection and extracted the very best for the book. At last the Mississippi Gulf Coast has a written history built on a hard base of primary material, most of which came directly from newspapers. It is hoped this first distillation will be only the tip of the iceberg. I am at present extracting from the Stevens collection the history of the hurricanes of the Mississippi Gulf Coast.

Prior to the airwaves and wire age, the written, or rather printed, word was the only means of mass communication—and that primarily via newspaper. Consequently, the newspaper served a far greater need in former times than it does now, and it did so splendidly. Ironically, in writing my book I had finer source material in the 19th century than in the 20th. Those wonderful letters faded from the newspapers with the coming of the telephone after the turn of the century. In the 1920s radio further depersonalized the newspapers, and television finished the job in the 1950s.

I do not know what wider application the findings presented here might portend for other areas, but newspapers saved the history of the Mississippi Gulf Coast. I can hardly believe, however, that the newspapers of New Orleans and Mobile were unique in their use of local correspondents. Other newspapers throughout the nation most likely did the same thing. For this reason, newspaper files are historical treasure troves. Archivists and librarians should treat them as such by expanding their holdings, and historians should recognize the value of newspaper collections by mining the historical gold and literary gems therein.

Newspapers Can Yield Genealogical Gems: One Amateur Genealogist's Experience

Larry L. Murdock

SUMMARY. This paper describes the use of newspapers by the author in searching out his family history. Hints are given about good sources of information and methods of going about procuring it. Many examples of personal experiences are included to illustrate the effectiveness of various approaches.

It's a fact: The columns of some old newspaper probably hold that crucial bit of information you need to break out of a long-standing bottleneck in your family history research. As you ponder it, however, finding that invaluable tidbit or datum would seem a discouraging task indeed. You imagine yourself pouring over stacks of yellowing, crumbling papers in the musty cellar of an aging archive. While scanning the papers you nervously glance from time to time toward a beetle-browed attendant, whose sanctuary you have violated and who glares crabbily at you over his spectacles.

It isn't a pleasant prospect. Additionally, other kinds of problems come to mind. Where do you find these old papers? What can you find in them? And how to direct your search once you've found them? Obviously, you could never read from cover to cover all the newspapers that might hold something of interest, you wouldn't live that long!

Happily, there are numerous fairly straight paths leading to newspaper that have valuable data on your ancestors. You must have the

---

Larry L. Murdock is a Professor of Entomology at Purdue University, Lafayette, Indiana. He holds a bachelor's degree from Depauw University and the PhD from Kansas State University. He has been interested in genealogical research for a number of years.

Editor's Note: This paper was solicited as a personal account of the author's experiences in using newspapers for genealogical research.

courage to stridle boldly down those paths, even when they seem only to lead into the genealogical underbrush. In this article, I shall recount some of my own experiences in those leafy thickets, in which you, too, can expect to find, from time to time, bright sunlit glades, where singing birds hover over long-sought genealogical gems. I am hoping that my experiences can serve as a guide. I hasten to add that I am an amateur genealogist only and that my experience with newspapers is limited and self-taught. There is an old Scottish proverb that says "he who teaches himsel' has a fule for a master." So much for my qualifications.

OBITUARIES REVIVE MORIBUND GENEALOGICAL RESEARCH — SCRAPS AND CLIPPINGS

One obvious source of information in newspapers is obituaries. My mother Dorothy's paternal grandfather, Asa Burdsall, was a Civil War veteran. Mother remembered him vividly, but her memories were those of a girl of fifteen, her age when he died. Girls of fifteen don't always remember the facts we genealogists want; and so while mother recalled colorful details about great-grandfather Asa, she could provide little vital data about him. Happily, however, she did somehow come into possession of a typewritten copy of Asa's obituary from a Lyons, Indiana, newspaper published in February, 1928. This was a lucky stroke, indeed, for the Lyons newspaper in question has long since closed its doors forever.

Asa's obituary provided a wealth of acts: (1) He was born in Tampico, Jackson County, Indiana, March 22, 1840 (the date is wrong by one year—but then don't believe everything you read in the newspapers); (2) His father was named James Burdsall, his mother Margaret Winn; (3) Asa enlisted in Company A, 50th Indiana Volunteer Regiment, at Vallonia, Indiana, and served three years; (4) After the Civil War he left Jackson County, coming to Lyons to stay with his sister, Mrs. Tom McKee; (5) He married Martha Landrum on January 29, 1874; (6) He and Martha had five children: Charles, Edward, Thornton, Oscar, and Rosa; (7) The couple took another child into their home to rear, who became Mrs. Thomas Lindsey; (8) Martha Landrum Burdsall died in 1909; after her death, Asa lived with his son, Edward, in Lyons; (9) Asa was a member of Mt. Zion Church of Christ; (10) His hearing failed in his last years; (11) He was held in high esteem in Lyons, for the obituary speaks of "the beauty of his character and disposition" and of the readiness of "his sunny smile and cheery word"; (12) He was survived by sons Charles and Edward of Lyons, Thornton of Gary, Indiana, Oscar of Indianapolis, by a daughter, Mrs. Rosa Paris of Trafalgar, Indiana, and by a sister, Mrs. Lucinda Beem of Lyons.

Asa's obituary is obviously a genealogist's treasure. Dates and major events of his life are all there. The names of his mother and father and children are given, as are the names of two of his sisters. On top of this, there is a glimpse into his character and personality. Even allowing for the sentimentality of small-town newspapers of half a century ago, Asa must have been a fine man.

My guess is that every one of us genealogists has ancestors for whom there exists, somewhere, similar excellent obituaries. The problem is: How do you find them? I could never have found Asa's obituary in a newspaper collection, for the paper in which his death notice appeared has long since been lost to neglect and corruption and the teeth of time. Fortunately, somebody cared enough to clip his obituary from the paper, and someone else made a transcript of it, and that copy finally landed in mother's hands. I'm certain that our ancestors and their relatives and friends have repeated this clipping and copying of obituaries millions of times over, and that there exists a vast but hidden and largely inaccessible collection of such genealogical gold coins, in bureau drawers and dusty scrapbooks all across the land. In small town America—and not so long ago America was predominantly small town and rural—it was always an honor to get your name in the local newspaper. Just about anyone who made the local front page one day invariably heard someone call out to the next, saying "Hey, I saw your name in the paper yesterday!" No matter why his name had made the paper, that individual knew he or she had just received a compliment.

Obituaries were final compliments in a slower, quieter America. They were clipped and saved and occasionally brought out into the light and read in the passing years by their aging collectors. So how do you find them? In old Bibles and long unopened books of elderly relatives. Folded into funeral cards and in cherished funeral-visitor books. In boxes of half-forgotten family papers, and in numerous other places as well. You can begin by asking Aunt Agnes if she has any. Likewise, don't neglect to enquire about them in your visits with Uncle Charlie and Aunt Hazel. Be explicit, too. Does he or she have any old newspaper clippings about . . . ?" A specific request may jar loose a forgotten memory, when a vague general request would fall upon deaf ears. If it should become your sad duty to clear up Great-Aunt Lizzie's estate, scrutinize carefully all papers in back drawers and in crumbling boxes before you discard their contents. Don't throw that obituary away! It may be the last copy in existence.

AGGRESSIVE OBITUARY FISHING: A HOW-TO GUIDE

Other sources of obituaries are the hundreds, even thousands, of newspaper collections, scattered across the country in county courthouses and in city, state, and national libraries, in the backrooms of little weeklies and dailies, and in the files and attics of unnumbered redbrick small-town Carnegie libraries. These collections are being discovered, catalogued, microfilmed, and made more accessible by various efforts such as those described elsewhere in this volume. My initiation into the mysteries of deliberate obituary seeking will illustrate in a general way how to go about using these collections. As often seems to be the case, a lucky incident got me started.

An early ancestor of mine was John McConnell. John came to the United States from County Antrim, Ireland, about 1805. He settled his large family in that part of northern Knox County, Indiana Territory, that subsequently became present-day Sullivan County. John's son, William, born April 1, 1816, was the grandfather of my great-grandmother Mary McConnell. Some years ago I knew of William's existence, but nothing more. Because I wanted to learn more about him and other Sullivan County ancestors, I joined the Sullivan County Historical Society, one of thousands of organizations dedicated to preserving local history. The $5.00 annual membership fee brought many benefits. Among them was a newsletter published at more or less regular intervals. There was an article that took my attention in the issue for September, 1982. In it, Harold W. Johnson, the newsletter editor, described a box of papers contributed to the Society. The box included a well-preserved copy of the *Sullivan Union*, for Wednesday, August 11, 1886. Johnson described some of the contents of the newspaper, and included a quote: "Uncle Billy McConnell, an old citizen of Haddon tp. died near Pleasantville August 4." I wrote Hal Johnson immediately, asking for more information. He replied promptly, sending a photocopy of the obituary notice. It mentioned William's Irish parentage. It went on to note that he was a fifty-year member of the Baptist church, but that for "advantages of farming" he had, shortly before his death, removed to adjacent Greene County. He was survived by a sister, Mrs. Betsy Gobin, of Carlisle. The obituary ends: "One by one the old pioneers are called away. . . ."

Although less rich than that of Asa Burdsall, William McConnell's obituary provided new and useful facts. More importantly, it proved conclusively that the dates on his gravestone are wrong! That stone is inscribed with the death date: August 8, 1887. The one-year discrepancy was explained when I later learned that the marker had been erected decades after William's death, by a grandson, who obviously had relied on a faulty source for his dates.

I got William McConnell's obituary more by luck than design, but obituaries can be found by deliberate search, as can notices of marriages, family reunions, and, in papers of more recent vintage, even births. I will consider only obituaries, but the principle of searching is the same for notices of other life events. You begin with, say, the death date of your great-great-grandmother. You might get this from your family Bible, from her tombstone, or from other family records. Knowing where she died is also important, as in most cases it will have been in her home locality, typically where she spent most of her adult life. You next determine whether there was a newspaper published at that time and place, of which there are copies or microfilms extant and available for searching. You find that newspaper, of course, using some of the approaches described elsewhere in this article and volume. The next step is to go to the library or archive having the newspapers and search them, beginning with issues a few days before the date of death—you may find mention that the person in question is ailing—and continuing for several days, even a week or two, afterwards. In older newspapers, obituaries may appear in many forms and on several different pages of the paper. These notices were not as systematically presented in past times as they are today. If the only available paper is a weekly, you should not fail to scan papers as late as several weeks after the death date—news didn't always travel as rapidly then as it does today. If you can't search the papers yourself, you may be able to find the name of a local genealogist who will do the job for you for a reasonable fee. Often, a local librarian can assist you or can put you in contact with someone to do the searching for you with a local historical or genealogical society that can help. In many cases, you will find the obituary you seek and learn who was present at the interment, who presided, and the circumstances of the death—a good return indeed for a little time and work. In short, find the date, find the place, find extant newspapers, and study them. You will be rewarded.

MORE FISHING FOR COUSINS, ANGLING FOR DESCENDANTS: PART TWO

When I was a kid growing up in Linton, Indiana, I was an avid bass fisherman. Surrounding the town were scores of old stripper pits, many of them large, in which lurked legendary seven- and eight-pound bigmouths. The barbershops of Linton were frequented by big mouths, too, of a different sort, not fish, but fishermen. In the spring and summer of the halcyon years of the mid-fifties, my biweekly visits to the barber, either Darwin Bank's place or Trusty Edward's, provided ample opportunity to drink in the fish stories. After years of listening and reflecting on innumerable yarns, it gradually dawned on me that the successful fisherman's secret was simple indeed: Go fishing often, in all kinds of weather, and in different places, and try a variety of baits and lures and methods. The anglers that keep at it are the ones who bring home the lunkers.

For most genealogists, current newspapers offer virgin waters for genealogical fishing. In 1980, as an amateur genealogist, I read (in a newspaper genealogical column, I believe) about a booklet listing current American newspapers that carried genealogical columns. For a small sum, perhaps $5.00, I soon had the booklet in my hand. It was compiled by Joyce Owen Metzger of Spokane, Washington. She listed more than 120 American and Canadian newspapers carrying genealogical columns, with names and addresses of the individual responsible for preparing the column. Mrs. Metzger, in introducing her list, urged the reader "never underestimate the power of the press—it works wonders."

What she says is true, of course, but this first came home to me when I tried my hand at it. A couple of examples will illustrate what you can expect by putting out your lines in current genealogical columns.

My third-great-grandfather, Joseph Landrum, emigrated from Halifax County, Virginia, to Owen County, Indiana, in 1821. I had reason to believe that his father was named Hawkins Landrum, but despite numerous letters to the helpful County Clerk of Halifax, I had been unable to learn much about Hawkins. Other than the fact that he was a minister (denomination unknown), he remained a shadowy figure. I very much wanted more information about him, but I was unsure about how to proceed. When Mrs. Metzger's booklet came to hand, I noted with interest that one of the newspapers listed was *The News and Record* of South Boston, Virginia, in the heart of Halifax County. The genealogical column it carried was "Halifacts," edited by one Kenneth Cook. I sent off the following query to Mr. Cook:

> I need information on the early Landrum family of Halifax County, especially HAWKINS LANDRUM, minister, whose son JOSEPH LANDRUM (1774-1861) moved to Owen County, Indiana, Indiana, in 1821. I also need information on Joseph's father-in-law, JOHN WYATT (WIATT), and his ancestors.

This little query brought in a whole string of genealogical facts and figures. My principal response came from Nathaniel Wooding, MD, of the town of Halifax. In addition to his family practice, Dr. Wooding is also the resident authority on the history of Halifax County, a non-stipendiary Episcopal priest and a fine amateur genealogist to boot. Mr. Wooding voluntarily searched records in the Halifax County courthouse for data on Hawkins Landrum and reported to me on his findings — in a detailed letter.

Among his discoveries were:

(i) That Hawkins was bonded to celebrate the rites of Holy Matrimony as a minister of the Society of Methodists, in 1784;

(ii) That Hawkins freed his slaves — following this lead I later obtained the document of manumission, which read: "Know all men by these presents that I Hawkins Landrum of Halifax County for divers good causes and considerations me thereunto moving and agreeable to an act of Assembly in that case made, and provided for Manumission of Slaves, do by these presents Emancipate and set free the following Negro Slaves (To Witt) Phill a Negro Man Aged a little upwards of twenty years to go free next Christmas from me, and Gowing a Negro Lad about fourteen years of age to be free from me at the age of Twenty One years and I do by these presents give up all my Rights and title claim and demand to the said slaves before mentioned and it is my desire that they enjoy all the immunities and liberties they as free men are entitled to by the laws of the land. Given under my hand and seal this 26th day of January 1789;

(iii) Reference to Hawkins' service as Inspector of Tobacco in Halifax County, a public office to which he was appointed by the governor;

(iv) The location of Hawkins' farm, which was on the Yellow Bank Branch and which abutted on "Wooding's Road,"

the Wooding in question being Dr. Nathaniel Wooding's fourth-great-grandfather, Col. Robert Wooding;
(v) A copy of Hawkins' handwritten will, which referred to his wife as "Sukey";
(vi) Evidence that Hawkins had come to Halifax from Buckingham County, Virginia.

Cook also replied to my query. Because of Cook's activities as a local historian and genealogist, he was aware of the existence of a Landrum family cemetery, with many old stones whose numerous inscriptions had not yet been recorded, — they still are not, but I hope to do the job myself one day, if someone else doesn't do it first. In addition, Clark put me in contact with an excellent local professional genealogist, Mrs. Lightfoot B. Farqurean, who systematically scoured the County Clerk's office for relevant data for me. By any standard, the yield in information from my little query was far more than I might have imagined — rather like catching a lunker fish with an inchworm.

Other queries placed in current genealogical columns have similarly yielded little treasures of data. In this way, I obtained the names and birthdates of all the children of Abraham Mitchell, a Revolutionary War veteran, who proved to be a fourth-great-grandfather. On another occasion, a query in a regional newspaper about Shake ancestors led to correspondence and later personal acquaintance with a third cousin, Mrs. Sarah Shake Snider, who had spent years gathering data on the Shake family. She generously shared her treasury of facts, and regularly keeps me up to date on progress in research on our common family line.

If you have reached a dead end with one of your family lines, you just might break the impasse by putting an enquiry into a genealogical column. This approach can work whether the ancestor lived in your present neighborhood or far away. Indeed, it may be especially useful for those ancestors who lived at a distance, as in this case fewer sources of information are easily available to the researcher. There are a number of ways to find the names and addresses of a genealogical column in your ancestor's neighborhood. One good way is to obtain the names of local or regional genealogical and historical societies near the locality of your ancestor. A letter to the society will usually bring the information you need. You might also scan the pages of recent issues of the *Genealogical Helper*, the premier popular genealogist's journal and a treasurehouse of information that sometimes includes listings of genealogical columns or pamphlets listing such columns. Another fine approach is to write to the librarian of the nearest local public library, using, by the way, the services of your local public library to help you find the needed library name and address. In my experience, librarians are invariably helpful, never failing to reply and usually providing useful information. Whatever route you take to find a local genealogical column, your newspaper query should give all of the essential information, i.e., the name(s) of the individual you are researching, the time period he or she was in the area, any data you have on the exact location (e.g., township, village, street), occupation, names of children or cousins, etc.

Failing a genealogical column, a useful alternative is to advertise for your ancestor in the personal column of the nearest local newspaper. This may cost a few dollars, but may pay disproportionate benefits.

SOME FURTHER HELP FROM LIBRARIANS

I can't keep myself from amplifying the foregoing point on the helpfulness of librarians, whom I consider to be a special, saintly form of humankind, created and fostered to help the rest of us. I won't name names, but I once wrote to a Sullivan County, Indiana, library to ask for data on my McConnell ancestors. The response was prompt and remarkable: three neatly-folded, single-spaced, narrow-margined pages, with not even a single typographical error, erasure, smudge or correction—pristinely hand-typed, obviously on a primitive mechanical typewriter! In immediate response to my query, this wonderful lady had made a typewritten transcript of every relevant line of information in her library, from books, pamphlets, and newspaper clippings. In trying to understand why she undertook such a typing chore in response to a mere mail enquiry, I could only assume that her photocopier must have been out of order.

On another occasion, I wrote to the Brazil, Indiana, Public Library to ask about newspaper holdings on microfilm. Within days, I had a typewritten listing of all holdings relevant to my query. This was most valuable, because it told me that the library had microfilm of the newspapers I needed to search, and it allowed me to plan my trip to Brazil so as to make the best use of my time there.

On still another occasion, when I appeared at the librarian's desk at Carlisle, Indiana, and asked for information on one of my ancestral family lines, the librarian picked up the phone, got a (then unknown) cousin on the line, and within minutes had me installed in the man's living room, discussing our common progenitors over a glass of iced tea. There's no doubt about it: librarians are America's most helpful and most undervalued people.

OTHER USES OF NEWSPAPERS

Names, birthdates, death dates, and marriage dates are the bare bones of genealogy. I personally don't care a lot about the bones themselves. I like, instead, to try to put them together and put flesh and skin on them and apply color to the cheeks of the people they represent. In this way, my ancestors come alive for me, and living ancestors are infinitely more interesting than dead bones. The raw materials for enlivening the bones of ancestors can be found in old newspapers. If you want to try an experiment in enlivening, you begin simply by finding a newspaper published in his or her locality in the appropriate period, and read several issues of it, as if you were a contemporary. Go through some issues from cover to cover, assuming citizenship of that time and place; read unhurriedly, looking over the advertisements and notices. After you understand the structure of the paper, skim and scan additional issues. You will be fascinated by what you discover. The prices of crops at the time your ancestor bought a farm, for example, would have been of great interest to that ancestor. Of much concern to him also would have been the burning of a local horse stable with all of its horses in it, or the prospect of a new railroad line passing near his farm. Other items of undoubted interest to him, especially if he were of draft age at the time, might include recruitment notices for the Civil War, the sinking of a coalmine shaft in the neighborhood, or the death of a pioneer resident.

I'll describe a few examples from my own newspaper research in order to give a better idea of what can be obtained in this way. An issue of the *Western Sun*, a pioneer newspaper published in Vincennes, Indiana, in the early years of the 19th century, described how Captain Andrew McConnell, brother of third-great-grandfather William McConnell, paraded his militia company at Carlisle, Indiana, on the Fourth of July, 1834. The vivid picture of patriotism and speeches evoked a sense of another time and place. It also conjured up the thought that William McConnell, being eighteen at the time, unmarried, and a younger brother, may have been one of the troops. Another issue of the same newspaper told me that Micajah Mayfield, a Revolutionary War veteran who was either my third-great-grandfather or the brother of my third-great-grandfather, was in Sullivan County, Indiana, in 1831, for there was a letter waiting for him at the Vincennes Post Office.

While scanning the *Brazil Times* for the year 1896, I discovered an occasional column describing happenings in the community of Cardonia, where my Murdoch ancestors settled after they emigrated from Scotland in 1890. It seemed that every other issue of the paper contained something relevant to these Murdochs, who, incidentally, were not local worthies but, rather, plain, tough coalmining folk. I was pleased, for example, to learn that the Scots of Cardonia continued to cherish the memory of Robert Burns, for they held a dinner in his honor on January 26, 1896, the dinner being well-attended, despite severe weather. In another issue I learned that my great-grandfather's brother, Alexander Murdoch, had, by the spring of 1896, already left Brazil and moved to Linton, Indiana, to work in the newly opened mines there. Another report mentioned that the mines in the Linton area had loaded 10,000 carloads of coal in the last year, and that production was limited only by a shortage of miners. In Wright township, northwest of Linton, a seam of coal, seven feet in thickness had been discovered, the thickest then known in the state of Indiana. This availability of jobs and the working out of the block coal seam around Brazil explained why the rest of the family, including my grandfather, removed to Linton in 1901. The very next issue of the *Brazil Times* described the marriage of Helen Murdoch, my great-grandfather's sister, to one George Smith, in Cardonia. This was a particularly valuable tidbit, because the marriage records for Clay County, Indiana, are in an imperfect state and carry no record for Helen Murdoch. An erroneous family tradition had it that Helen had married someone named Hunter instead. These examples are enough to suggest some of the predictable and unpredictable rewards of scanning local papers.

You don't have to restrict your newspaper reading to local dailies and weeklies, however, I have found many items of direct relevance to my own family history in the *New York Times*—again I stress that none of my ancestors were rich, famous, or infamous—and I think it fairly certain that just about every American can find things of interest in this and other big city papers. One reason to consider them is easy availability. Large metropolitan newspapers like the *New York Times* are widely available on microfilm in many university and college libraries as well as in state libraries and in larger city libraries. For example, scanning the *New York Times* for October, 1886, revealed the price of passage from Glasgow, Scotland, to New York City, on the *State of Georgia*, the ship that carried my great-grandfather to America for the first time. I could get a fair idea of what their journey had cost. Another example: The *New York Times* for mid- and late September, 1863, described the tension and confused events leading up to the capture of the Union garrison at Munfordville, Kentucky, by Confederate troops under General Braxton Bragg. Great-grandfather Asa Burdsall, whose regiment had been sent to relieve the Munfordville garrison, was among the 5,000 Union soldiers captured. By reading these papers I could vividly appreciate what was happening to him at the time, and what thoughts and concerns must then have been passing through his mind.

The examples could go on and on. Simply by reading and scanning old newspapers you can gain a sense of time and place, an appreciation of values and concerns of the people, a knowledge of long-forgotten but once important local happenings — genealogical color you can get in no other way.

AN EXCELLENT RESOURCE

If you want more detailed ideas and guidance about finding and using newspapers for genealogical research, I suggest you go to the nearest library and obtain a copy of the *The Source: A Guidebook of American Genealogy*, edited by Arlene Eakle and Johni Cerny. Published by Ancestry Publishing Company, Salt Lake City, Utah, in 1984, this 786-page book is an excellent general genealogical resource. Chapter 12, on newspapers, by Loretto Dennis Szucs, presents in twenty pages an abundance of valuable facts and guidance on the availability and use of newspapers in genealogical research.

Military Newspapers: A Brief Overview

Robert C. Boots

SUMMARY. This article discusses the creation and use by the military of a special current awareness tool called *Current News*. This publication, which is produced daily from a variety of news sources, identifies and transmits through military communication channels stories that are of particular interest to the Department of Defense installations. Other publications and the roles they have played or are currently playing in the military information community are also mentioned.

In 1870 General William B. Hazen of the U.S. Army traveled to France, where he observed the disastrous defeat of the French army by the North German Confederation. The French army was essentially a highly paid mercenary organization, while the German army was drawn from all levels of society. General Hazen made this telling observation, ". . . an army, to be of value, must possess the true national spirit of its time, and be allied in sympathy with the people; otherwise the profession of arms is reduced to a mere trade, and becomes an incubus and a danger . . . " How is this to be avoided?

An obvious avenue whereby the military can keep abreast of the national spirit is through the media, and most notably the country's newspapers. Today all high level commands are updated on this spirit through a unique publication entitled *Current News*. This publication is issued by the Office of the Secretary of the Air Force, Current News Branch, located at the Pentagon. It is distributed daily through military communications channels. Until January, 1986, it was issued in three editions, the Early Bird, which appeared between 6:00 and 6:30 a.m. in the eastern U.S.; the Current News edition, which came out at midday; and an edition dealing with special topics that was published as needed. Now, because of budget constraints, it has been reduced to

---

Robert Boots holds a BA from Indiana State University and an MA from Pennsylvania State University. He currently holds the position of historian in the Air Force Systems Division, Air Force Wright Aeronautical Laboratories, Wright-Patterson AFB, Dayton, OH.

one edition, the Early Bird. Upon receipt at the various Department of Defense installations, this publication often has added to it articles from local and regional newspapers that are of particular interest to the installation.

An examination of the Early Bird edition of March 11, 1986, *Current News* reveals this newspaper's complex make-up. The articles in this issue were taken from the *New York Times*, the *Washington Post*, the *Washington Times*, *Common Cause Magazine*, the *St. Louis Post-Dispatch*, the *St. Louis Globe-Democrat*, *U.S. News and World Report*, *Time*, the *Chicago Tribune*, and the *Baltimore News-American*. These articles appear with full source citations, and are formatted as they appeared in the originating publication. Thy deal with U.S. dependence on Japan for spare parts, U.S. aid to the Nicaraguan rebels, sale of advanced missiles to Saudi Arabia, the Iran-Iraq war, the need for an atomic test-ban treaty with the U.S.S.R., negotiations between the U.S. and West Germany concerning "star wars," the current level of military spending and military insecurity, and so on. The articles that appear are selected by the News Clippings and Analysis Service of the Current News Branch.

Current News began as a strictly Air Force publication in 1950. At that time each individual service had its Washington, D.C., public affairs office prepare a similar, though less elaborate, synopsis of newspaper articles. These tended to be oriented toward the particular service preparing the synopsis and limited to items from Washington, D.C., and New York papers. In 1963 Secretary of Defense Robert MacNamara, to improve the efficiency and economy of the operation, placed responsibility for this function solely under the jurisdiction of the Secretary of the Air Force. The purpose of *Current News* has always been to make available to high level Department of Defense officials comments for use in the decision making process on significant national defense issues.

Current News is not readily available to some service members, but there are newspapers that cater directly to the informational needs of all. The *Army Times*, the *Navy Times*, and the *Air Force Times* are weekly newspapers distributed world-wide to military personnel through subscription. They are also available at base and post exchanges. These newspapers are published on Monday of each week by the Army Times Publishing Company, a division of the Times Journal Company, Springfield, Virginia. Though they include some editorial content from other newspapers, much is original. In each, moreover, a letters to the editor section is provided so that service members can express their views on current national and service-related topics.

The *Army Times* dates from 1940, but its origins are to be found in preceding publications. The *Army-Navy Journal*, which started publication on a weekly basis in 1863, was a private enterprise catering to a military audience. This newspaper was published in New York City by William C. Church, who in 1865 was joined by his brother Frederick. A detailed biographical study of the Churches and the early years of the *Army-Navy Journal* can be found in the work of Donald N. Bigelow, *William C. Church and the Army-Navy Journal*, Columbia University Press, New York, 1952. This weekly newspaper kept the isolated soldier stationed in the "great American desert" abreast of events of service, national and international interest. The *Army-Navy Journal* was a curious mix of the *Current News*, the *Army Times*, and the hometown classified advertising section.

In addition to material produced by its own staff, the *Army-Navy Journal* contained copy reprinted from other newspapers that dealt with military and political questions of importance. It had an extensive and lively letters section as well as comprehensive articles written by service members on military and social topics. During the Franco-Prussian War, which General Hazen had gone to observe, the *Army-Navy Journal* published accounts from English, French, and German newspapers concerning not only the military aspects of the conflict but also its political implications. Before the Spanish-American War, when "yellow journalism" was running rampant, the editorial pages of this publication were filled with cautions concerning the various aspects of mobilizing the nation for war. Its balanced and informative news digest continued to serve the armed services until 1965.

The *Army-Navy Journal* was soon to share its privileged position as a news source for the armed services. Debate was taking place before the outbreak of the Franco-Prussian War concerning all aspects of the American military establishment. This included a consideration of enlisted personnel and officer education, conscription, staff organizations, pay and entitlements, funding and the purpose of a military organization in a democratic nation during peace. The example of an efficient and cost-effective military organization such as that of Count von Miltke's Prussian Army, as contrasted with the wasteful and disorganized northern forces at the outset of the American Civil War, added fuel to the discussion. The debate reached a high pitch during the late 1870s when Senator Ambrose Burnside of Rhode Island chaired a congressional committee considering a reform of the American military establishment. Supported by military reformers such as a General William Tecumseh Sherman and Colonel Emory Upton, the Burnside Committee faced stern opposition from the "established" military bureaucracy in Washington. The *Army-Navy Journal* supported the efforts of the Burnside Committee and the reformers. Then, on December 13, 1879, the *Army-Navy Register* made its appearance. The fact that it was published privately in Washington, D.C., may account for its initial editorial tone in support of the "status quo" of the American military establishment. Yet in basic format and content the *Army-Navy Journal* and the *Army-Navy Register* were nearly identical. It is a final irony that these two weekly newspapers would merge in 1965 to form the *Journal of the Armed Forces*, which has since been renamed the *Journal of the Armed Forces International*.

The need for an intelligent military in a democratic republic was clearly stated by General Hazen, and has been reiterated thousands of times since. There exists within the armed services a clear commitment to keeping in touch with the feelings of the society they are sworn to defend. Newspapers, then, can be said to keep military leaders informed about the nation's "spirit."

Other publications, such as those printed by the U.S. Army, have likewise provided useful sources of information. Among these are the *Military Review*, and *Parameters: Journal of the U.S. Army War College*, as well as the privately published *Jane's Defense Weekly*. These publications tend to run scholarly or internationally oriented articles, and are not published in traditional newspaper format. Nevertheless, the best source used by the military to keep in touch with what is happening in the world is the newspaper. Because of its diverse character and timeliness, the newspaper provides a valuable tool for policy making and education in the armed services, and helps the military to avoid ever becoming ". . . an incubus and a danger . . ."

International Newspaper Considerations

Hana Komorous

SUMMARY. Current international developments in the field of newspaper librarianship and preservation are discussed. The existence of various national newspaper programs is pointed out, and the Canadian nation-wide plan described. Activities of the IFLA Working Group on Newspapers are outlined, and its major projects analyzed.

INTRODUCTION

Ti-pao, the Chinese handwritten paper of the Han dynasty, *Acta Diurna Populi Romani* of the Roman Empire, the Mexican newsheet *Relación del Terremoto de Guatemala*, Boston's *Publick Occurencies* and Australia's *Sydney Gazette* are examples that illustrate the international origins of the newspaper over a period extending from the second century B.C. to 1803. Since then, the development of the world press has proceeded from newspapers published on newsprint all the way to the electronic newspaper.

Nations on all continents have tried to collect and preserve their newspapers in national and local repositories; but it is only in the past two decades that an intensified interest has arisen in newspaper collecting and preservation, and this has brought progress in solving some of the major problems that newspaper repositories experience. It was soon apparent, of course, that these problems could not be solved by individual institutions at the local level alone, and in consequence many national programs emerged. National and international advances in the field of preservation in general, the impact of library automation, and developments in preservation technologies were, in general, the concerns dealt with in these programs. While the historical background, scope, approach and organization of individual national pro-

---

Hana Komorous MA, MLS, is Senior Serials Librarian, McPherson Library, University of Victoria, British Columbia and Project Manager, British Columbia Newspaper Project. She has been a member of the IFLA Working Group on Newspapers since 1982.

grams differ, the major issues they address do not. Problems of collection, preservation and access to newspapers are all being examined. Australia, Canada, Finland, France, Great Britain, New Zealand, Sweden and the United States are among the countries that have national policies for the preservation of their newspapers, or are in process of formulating such policies.

CANADIAN NATION-WIDE PLAN

In Canada, the nation-wide plan for the preservation of Canadian newspapers was initiated by the National Library. This program known, as the Decentralized Program for Canadian Newspaper Preservation and Access, was formulated in 1982 by the Resource Network Committee of the National Library Advisory Board. It is designed multi-jurisdictional model program, the purpose of which is to delineate the roles and responsibilities of both federal and provincial agencies in newspaper preservation. While the National Library is responsible for overall coordination and planning, the provinces and territories have been asked to formulate plans for collecting, preserving and providing access to their own newspapers and for compiling checklists of all current and retrospective provincial newspapers.[1] The National Library has provided the individual provincial projects with seed money for planning and conducting inventories.

The progress of the program was summarized at the National Newspapers Colloquium convened by the National Library on November 12 and 13, 1985, in Ottawa.[2] This colloquium provided the provinces and territories participating in the Decentralized Program with a forum for reporting their activities and progress, for bringing up problems and concerns, and for exchanging opinions. Twelve presentations were made, in which the diversity and variety of the various programs were revealed. Presentations were made also on such topics as preservation, physical access, intellectual access and the future of the Decentralized Program for Canadian Newspapers. Major problems were thus identified, and first steps in their solution proposed:

> In the matter of bibliographic control, the need for standardization was expressed. This resulted in the establishment of the Technical Services Working Group which will propose minimum standards for newspaper records.
> In that of preservation microfilming, problems of funding, standards and copyright were discussed. The National Library proposed to buy one positive copy of each microfilmed Canadian

newspaper for purposes of security, research, and interprovincial interlibrary loan. Provincial and territorial representatives left Ottawa with the assignment to consider the question of provincial repositories of service copies and microform masters, and to discuss the safe storage of masters and the production of intermediaries. A policy for the retention of originals after microfilming was proposed and will be discussed by the provinces and territories. The National Library will set up a working group to consider guidelines for the storage, handling and treatment of original issues.

In the matter of intellectual access, the participants were in agreement that a comprehensive listing of all Canadian newspapers in machine-readable form, available online and in COM format, should be the final finding tool. Problems of ongoing indexing projects were discussed and a need for the development of guidelines and thesauri for Canadian subjects expressed. In addition, the provinces and territories were asked to consider what holdings should be included in the national union list.

It can be said that Canada's national newspaper program has been planned, and is progressing in a distinctively Canadian manner. Regional diversities are recognized while common elements are promoted. The program should bring a successful confederation of Canadian newspaper projects and, in the long term, assure the preservation of Canadian newspapers.[3]

IFLA WORKING GROUP ON NEWSPAPERS

While the task of inventorying, preserving and accessing newspapers must be undertaken at the national level, the feeling is that collectively this task should be regarded as an international obligation. Recognizing this need, the International Federation of Library Associations and Institutions (IFLA) established the Working Group on Newspapers (WGN). The Group which was formed under the auspices of IFLA's Section on Serial Publications, held its first meeting in the Staatsbibliothek Preussischer Kulturbesitz, Berlin on May 14th, 1980.[4] The three founding members were newspaper specialists from Germany, Great Britain and Sweden. The working plan formulated at the first meeting included a consideration of: newspaper definitions, national newspaper collection surveys and international standardization.[5] Since the Berlin meeting, the Group has made commendable progress. At present it has thirteen members and seven observers, who collectively represent an expert knowledge of newspaper topics. The members and observers are from seven European countries, Canada, the United States, New Zealand and South Africa. To date nine meetings have been held, all in Europe, the latest one on April 10-11, 1986, in Vienna. The working plans have been expanded and, despite problems caused by the inability of some members to attend meetings, substantial progress has been made.

As in the national programs, the considerations addressed by the WGN encompass the following areas:

— collection
— access
— preservation
— standardization

COLLECTION

The Survey of National Newspaper Collections was the first project initiated by the Group. Two questionnaires were drawn up and sent at staggered intervals to 359 libraries, archives and other institutions in 151 countries. The twenty-nine questions in the questionnaires dealt with the definition of a newspaper, newspaper acquisition policies, newspaper microfilming, copyright restrictions, interlending of newspapers in microform and the existence of printed and non-printed national newspaper catalogs. The aim of the survey was to collect data needed for an overview of the treatment of newspapers at the national level.

Over 30% of the questionnaires were returned. Respondents from Europe, Africa, Asia, North America, South America, Australia and Oceania were represented. The project is being carried out by two members of the Working Group, Willi Höfig, Staatsbibliothek Preussischer Kulturbesitz, Berlin, and Johan Mannerheim, Kungliga Biblioteket, Stockholm. Results of the survey are being analyzed; and once a detailed report is presented for the consideration of the Group, decisions will be made about the format and content of the final publication(s).

ACCESS

The WGN has held discussions concerning physical access to newspapers. These discussions have focused on problems of international interlibrary lending. In terms of intellectual access to newspapers, the

Group's activity concentrated on the compilation of the *International Guidelines for the Cataloging of Newspapers*. The first draft was prepared by Robert Harriman of the Library of Congress and Hana Komorous of the University of Victoria in cooperation with Mary S. Price of the Library of Congress. It is anticipated that when the final version is approved and published, the guidelines will be used for:

— Current and retrospective cataloging of newspaper collections.
— Compiling union lists of newspapers.
— Entering newspaper records into database facilities.
— International exchanging of newspaper bibliographic records.
— Compiling newspaper bibliographies and specialized lists.[6]

PRESERVATION

The Newspaper Conservation Project is the major project undertaken by the WGN in the field of preservation. Mme. Peraud of the Bibliothèque Nationale, Paris, is the project's director. A questionnaire distributed world-wide is being used to collect the following:

— Description of newspaper microfilm collections of individual institutions.
— Information on management and staffing of these collections.
— Information on microfilm equipment and its maintenance.
— Information on user services, including existence of catalogs to these collections and the means, if any, of updating these catalogs.
— Information on preservation of the microfilm collection, including storage conditions.
— Information on maintenance of microforms in the collection.

Data collected by means of this questionnaire will be summarized and reported by Mme. Peraud to the Group for discussion and later dissemination to other IFLA sections.

STANDARDIZATION

In its endeavor to cover problems of newspaper librarianship from the international perspective and to find solutions to these that can be applied in a world-wide sense, the WGN has been involved in the formulation and revision of international standards. The Group's discussions have been focused on standards concerning the storage of original newspapers and newspapers in microform, the microfilming of newspapers, and newspaper related definitions. In particular, the revision of the International Organization for Standardization (ISO) standard 4087-1979, the *Microfilming of Newspapers on 35 mm Unperforated Microfilm for Archival Purposes* has been discussed in detail.

The definition of a newspaper and definitions of newspaper editions have been on the WGN agenda since its first meeting. The final definition of a newspaper was approved by the Group and accepted by ISO. It reads as follows:

> Newspaper: Serial publication which contains news on current events of special or general interest, the individual parts of which are listed chronologically or numerically and appear usually at least once a week. NOTE — Newspapers usually appear without a cover, with a masthead, are normally printed on newsprint and are normally larger than A3 (297mm × 420mm) in size.

INTERNATIONAL SYMPOSIUM ON NEWSPAPERS

In 1983 the IFLA Working Group on Newspapers undertook the planning of an international newspapers symposium, and has held preliminary discussions on its purposes and content. The reasons for holding the symposium have been defined as follows:

- For many years, newspapers in libraries have been neglected. Recently their importance has been recognized by librarians and user communities at both the national and international level.
- As significant activity concerning newspaper collections is taking place at the national level, a broadly-based international symposium would promote an exchange of experiences.
- To maximize the benefits of the proceedings of the IFLA Working Group on Newspapers, conclusions arrived at by the Group should be presented to a wider audience, thus encouraging more countries to treat seriously the problems posed by their newspaper collections.

At the time of this writing the planning of the symposium is approaching its final stages. The symposium will be held in August, 1987, in Brighton, England, as a pre-conference symposium to the main IFLA Conference.

CONCLUSION

The international developments in newspaper librarianship described in this article illustrate only a small portion of current worldwide activities in this field. As national and international projects progress, making more information available and the exchange of experiences possible, the ultimate goal — preservation of the world's newspapers as a collective heritage — will come closer to realization.

NOTES AND REFERENCES

1. National Library Advisory Board, Resource Network Committee, A Decentralized Program for Canadian Newspaper Preservation and Access (Ottawa, December 1982).
2. "National Newspapers Colloquium." National Library News 18, no. 1 (Jan. 1986): 1-2, 8.
3. The description of the National Newspapers Colloquium is based on a draft report prepared by the National Library in April 1986.
4. An earlier IFLA Newspaper Group, convened in 1969, had slightly different orientation than the current WGN.
5. Hofig, Willi. "Report of the IFLA Working Group on Newspapers." IFLA Annual (1981): 211-12.
6. Komorous, Hana and Harriman, Robert. International Guidelines for the Cataloguing of Newspapers. Prepared for the IFLA Working Group on Newspapers. First draft (March 1986).
7. In addition to the cited sources, the description of projects and activities of the IFLA Working Group on Newspapers is based on Minutes of the Group's meeting and on personal notes and correspondence of the author.

A Selective Overview of Newspaper Indexes – 1986

Edward D. Starkey

SUMMARY. Indexes for major newspapers are available today in a variety of published formats, all generated from automated databases. Printed indexes, both on paper and on microfilm, continue to be useful. Self-contained automated indexing systems using optical disc technology are now appearing in libraries. Finally, online access to indexes and the text of newspapers is a rapidly growing practice.

"Newspapers are the first rough draft of history." So stated the late Philip Graham, publisher of *The Washington Post*.[1] Newspapers, when collected retrospectively, indeed contain vast amounts of material of historical value. Unfortunately this material is all but inaccessible if it is not indexed in some manner. The earliest attempts to index newspapers of research importance were made in the mid-nineteenth century. *The Times* of London of this era can be accessed through *Palmer's Index to The Times Newspaper*, which was begun in 1867 but carried retrospectively back to 1791. Thus, any American reader with access to a larger research library has direct reporting on the French Revolution and the Napoleonic wars.

Many newspapers in North America have been indexed locally, often with card or "shoebox" systems. Some such local indexes have been published in printed format. Kenneth Sell identified twenty-nine available in the seventies.[2]

The advent of automation has changed newspaper indexing radically. Although still labor intensive – until 1983 *The New York Times* employed 120 persons in its indexing department – indexing is now more accurate and versatile than ever before, and is available in a variety of published formats. Today all indexing of major regional and

---

Edward D. Starkey is head of public services at the University Library, Indiana University-Purdue University at Indianapolis, 815 West Michigan Street, Indianapolis, IN 46202. He holds a bachelor's degree and three master's degrees, including the MSLS, from the University of Kentucky.

national newspapers is computerized. The difference between indexes lies largely in output format. Some are printed in traditional book format, one is on microfilm, a few are available in self-contained automated systems, and many are accessible online.

What is most characteristic of automated indexing is change. New formats and new indexes become available not yearly, but several times yearly. It is therefore worthwhile to offer an overview of the scene every several years.[3]

The dean of American newspaper indexes is *The New York Times Index*, which covers the entire run of the paper from its first issues in 1851. For the first seven years of publication, the index is a reproduction of handwritten entries, some very colorful: "affray between Cohen and King" and "Indian outrages." By late 1858 a printed version appeared, and the index grew in sophistication throughout the nineteenth century. Now it presents abstracts of news, editorials and features arranged under its own subject headings. As a reference work, it transcends its indexing value. Abstracts on a particular issue can be followed in the index and thus the reader can gain a chronological overview without resorting to the microfilmed paper itself. In fact, if a library has this index alone, it can be used by the patron in establishing dates and other authority information that will be helpful in consulting the local paper. Until 1982 graphs, maps and photographs were included, enhancing the reference value. Indexing in the early seventies was particularly full, and the work grew by 1975 to 2800 pages bound in two volumes. In 1976 the single volume format was reestablished, and the page count dropped to 1800.

Although *The New York Times* is not a national newspaper for the United States in the sense that *Le Monde* is for France, even its critics concede that it is one of the keystones of North American journalism, and in fact most public and academic libraries have a current subscription, a back run on microfilm and the index. The danger lies in taking too seriously the *Times'* claim to be the newspaper of record for the country and overlooking other newspapers of national stature and regional importance.

Bell & Howell helps libraries avoid this mistake by providing printed indexes for ten newspapers of regional importance; two for national newspapers, *The Christian Science Monitor* and *USA Today*; and eleven for Black newspapers such as New York's *Amsterdam News*.[4] These indexes are divided into two alphabets, one arranged by subject and the other by personal name. Most of these indexes were begun in the late seventies and were reproduced in the gruesome computer printout of the day. Readability mellowed to an acceptable boldface in 1980, and advanced to the truly eye-pleasing with the 1985 editions. Though brief abstracts were added in the eighties, these indexes do not approach in their reference usefulness *The New York Times Index*. With them, however, any library can have coverage for its own region as well as access to some national news.

These indexes can be searched online through Bell & Howell's *NDEX*, available on SDC's ORBIT. A word of warning, however: a few newspapers were dropped by Bell & Howell in the early eighties. Indexing for these, whether in print or online, covers only a few years and is long out of date.

Like the Bell & Howell indexes, *The Wall Street Journal Index* is divided into two sections. Corporate news is found in the first section arranged by company name, and general news is indexed under the *Journal*'s own terms in the second. This index first appeared in 1958, and is essential for any library serving a business community.

A rather different printed indexing system is *NewsBank*, which offers libraries an index updated monthly and cumulated quarterly and annually to articles taken from newspapers published in all fifty states. These articles are available to *NewsBank* subscribers on microfiche, which are stored by broad subject areas. The researcher has readily available an enormous amount of material (100,000 items are added annually), thoroughly indexed, at less expense than with the fulltext online systems to be described below. No one newspaper, however, is entirely indexed. Some librarians argue that the microfiche format of the articles will turn patrons away, but short of online fulltext retrieval, all newspaper indexing ultimately sends the reader to microforms. *NewsBank*, then, is a package of newspaper articles with indexing that is successfully used in libraries of all types. Its indexes have become available on an automated, self-contained system, *NewsBank Electronic Index*, to be described below.

In searching for current information in newspapers, the librarian may well turn to *Facts on File* (1941-) and its younger sister *Editorials on File* (1970-). *Facts on File* can make a good claim to being more accurate than newspapers because its weekly updates are written a few days after events, when there has been more time for sources to be checked and editorial decisions to be made on what is significant. The material in the weekly editions is provided with good indexes, which are cumulated throughout the year. For up-to-date information the service can be accessed online as *Facts on File World News Digest* through DIALOG, NEXIS AND VU/TEXT. *Keesing's Contemporary Archives* (1931-) is a similar British offering.

These printed indexes offer the advantages of being available to patrons free of charge and of accessibility without the need for special training. They readily invite browsing, the oldest searching technique of the curious. They will drop out of publication only when user-friendly machines providing the same or more information are available widely and without cost to the patron.

Printed indexes sold commercially to libraries continue to be important in spite of advances in computer technology that make machine-readable indexing available either online or in closed systems. Indeed, all printed indexes sold today are produced from databases, and it is computer technology that has increased their possibilities. They offer one truly great advantage over automated indexes. Once they are bought with library funds, there is no debate about the patron's free access to them. No public or academic library in North America charges patrons to use the printed *New York Times Index*, but many would charge for using the *Times* and its index online.

The National Newspaper Index, produced by the Information Access Corporation, may be considered a halfway point between printed and online indexes. Printed indeed it is, but on microfilm, and a motor driven reader presents the patron with indexing for *The Wall Street Journal*, *The New York Times*, and *The Christian Science Monitor* from 1979 and for *The Washington Post* and the *Los Angeles Times* from late 1982. Subjects, titles and authors are supplied in a single alphabet, and the index is newly cumulated and sent to libraries each month.

As with any printed index, the time-lag grows greater as the month wears on. This gap can be filled by searching Information Access' *NewSearch* online via DIALOG or BRS. This is updated every twenty-four hours, and contains the current month of *The National Newspaper Index* as well as updates of other Information Access databases.

Information Access also produced *InfoTrac* and with this fully automated—but not online—recovery of information is achieved.[5] *InfoTrac* contains indexing to some 800 periodicals, including a projected year of *The Wall Street Journal* and two months of *The New York Times*. The information is placed on an optical disc, and retrieved by patrons using IBM personal computers. The system is a model of user-friendliness, and seems positively to draw patrons to it. When citations are found under a subject entry, they can at once be run off on a printer connected to the computer. One does not, of course, achieve bibliographic nirvana after a few minutes at *InfoTrac*. Serious researchers need to do much further searching in scholarly indexes and bibliographies if they are to produce reports and papers of acceptable quality, but a common misunderstanding of this cannot be held against *InfoTrac*. A more serious problem is the primitive searching technique that is prescribed. Terms cannot be linked by Boolean operators,* and one often has to wade through a host of screens to find the subdivision on a subject one needs. This drawback exists also in the use of printed indexes. A library subscribing to the printed indexes of the *Times* and the *Journal* and *InfoTrac* will, however, find that a good deal of the indexing time-lag is filled by *InfoTrac*, while the printed updates are awaited.

InfoTrac will be looked upon as transitional in the not-too-distant future. Searching techniques will have to be made more sophisticated. In addition to the great advantage of access through a personal computer with a printer attached to it—a mode of study and communication for an increasing number of people—there is the advantage of cost effectiveness. The hardware is indeed expensive, in the neighborhood of $20,000 per year for four computers and printers and the accompanying optical disc equipment and monthly cumulated discs, until after five years the hardware is owned by the purchaser. There are, however, no communications or usage charges, as there are with online systems, and once the system is in place any number of searches can be performed without the paying of additional fees.

It is not the purpose of this paper to cover the differences between the various technological options for self-contained bibliographic databases, but there does seem to be a preponderance of opinion in favor of the more compact CD/ROM optical disc technology, as opposed to *InfoTrac*'s 12-inch laser disc. It is with CD/ROM for instance, that *NewsBank* has just made available its indexes for automated searching.

The *NewsBank Electronic Index* is similar to *InfoTrac* in that the index is cumulated monthly. *InfoTrac*, attractive as it is to patrons, however, produces a high level of frustration immediately after use. It indexes approximately 800 periodicals, many of them popular and trade publications, and even large libraries have a limited subscription list for these. The *NewsBank* system avoids this patron frustration through its system of providing on fiche every article it indexes. *NewsBank* also allows a more sophisticated searching technique by reason of its hierarchical subject format and the device of giving article counts when subject headings are entered.

With communications charges increasing, electronic, self-contained

---

***Editor's Note**: Boolean operators give the user the ability to combine and/or exclude terms while searching, and thus to make the activity more efficient.

systems are an attractive option for indexes of many varieties. Of course, the great disadvantage of monthly updates is that at any given moment the information in the index is from two to six weeks old—a weakness that can be overcome only by going online.

One issue about which the library community will have to be very vocal is compatibility. It is all well and good for a company to sell libraries dedicated hardware such as Information Access has done with *InfoTrac*, but what happens when several companies offer products without which one "cannot live," but each of which uses dedicated and expensive hardware? Both *NewsBank Electronic Index* and *InfoTrac* are accessible by IBM personal computers, but there is at the moment no way to access both of these databases from the same computer.

The New York Times, as noted, produced the first American printed index of national importance. So also it produced one of the first online indexes. Begun in the mid-sixties, The New York Times Information Service first marketed in 1972 an online index of the newspaper in its *Information Bank*.[6] Among its first customers were government agencies and libraries. Although there were problems with the indexing, it rapidly became an information staple as a new specialty emerged in libraries—online searching.

In 1983 the *Times* made the decision to withdraw from marketing this database. It signed an exclusive contract with Mead Data Central to make it available through NEXIS along with the full text of the daily paper from 1980 onwards. This caused some consternation in the information field since NEXIS was then available only over dedicated terminals, and librarians had grown used to searching a number of systems through the same machine. Mead has since changed its policy and moved away from the use of dedicated terminals, and NEXIS can now be accessed with Mead software from most terminals in use in libraries. NEXIS remains the exclusive purveyor of the fulltext *Times* and the *Information Bank* system, which includes indexing of the paper and some sixty other periodicals. This indexing continues to be created by *Times* staff members. NEXIS also offers fulltext retrieval of *The Christian Science Monitor*, *The Washington Post*, and the *Los Angeles Times*. Although the hurdle of the dedicated terminal has been surmounted, relatively few academic and public libraries subscribe to NEXIS. High cost is the deciding factor. At this time, Mead does not have an active program of marketing to these libraries, although in the future it may allow consortium subscriptions so that costs can be shared by groups of libraries. It is indeed ironic that the publication that considers itself to be the national newspaper of record has arranged for its text and indexing to be unavailable to most libraries in technologically advanced format, when, as it shall be seen, many other papers are easily and inexpensively accessible, and competitive indexing services like *The National Newspaper Index* provide indexing of the *Times*.

The creation of computer databases for the typesetting of newspapers gives advantages other than more accurate and speedy printing. When a database exists, the newspaper can be stored in electronic format indefinitely, descriptors can be added to the articles, and the text can be scanned as needed by reporters and researchers. The newspaper that first became available in this fashion was *The Toronto Globe and Mail*. Its *Info Globe* system came online in 1977. The addition of descriptors and the availability of the text to random access freetext searching qualifies such databases as combination indexes-with-sources. Until newspapers became available online, the only electronic transfer of up-to-date information was through audio or video systems.

Networks were created to make newspaper output available. VU/TEXT began as an internal library for the two Philadelphia Knight-Ridder newspapers, the *Daily News* and the *Inquirer*.[7] The parent company realized the broader value of databases such as its own, and set up VU/TEXT as a separate division to make available the full text of many newspapers. By the summer of 1985 VU/TEXT offered fifteen papers, and a year later almost forty, representing every region in the nation. Of particular significance is the availability of the AP wire service. A search of VU/TEXT for this wire service will not only bring in information that is up-to-date but also up-to-the-hour. Descriptors are added to facilitate searching, but there is not available as yet the sort of advanced indexing provided by *The New York Times*.

DataTimes, produced by the DataTek Corporation, began similarly as an in-house archival system for *The Daily Oklahoman*, and has grown since its founding in 1981 into a fulltext service for twelve newspapers with four more soon to come online.[8] DataTimes also offers the AP and Southwest wire services fulltext.

As of the summer of 1986, commercial newspaper indexing is offered to libraries in a variety of formats, accessible by both librarian and patron. Further, there is every prospect that more newspapers will be available via online fulltext services. Neither *The New York Times* nor Bell & Howell show any signs, however, of giving up their paper indexes, and indeed many libraries would be seriously inconvenienced without them. It is interesting to note in this connection that Bell &

Howell has actually increased the number and quality of its printed indexes over the past ten years.

Indexes printed on paper will continue to be used as reference books in themselves, will continue to be especially useful for browsing, and will continue to be offered in the longstanding tradition of no-fee service.

One other factor to consider is storage cost. A daily newspaper contains an enormous amount of data and to keep it available online or on a readily accessible optical disc is expensive. It is entirely probable that automated systems will continue to produce a variety of published formats. Online or optical disc output will be available for searching recent years, and paper indexes will be printed for retrospective indexing of microform copies of the paper.

Databases that can be accessed online via terminals or microcomputers will go on being used by those who can afford the telecommunications costs. For the searcher in the corporate library, this may be considered a cheap means of obtaining information. If telecommunications costs continue to rise, however, use of online databases may decline, as patrons will find it increasingly difficult to pay online charges.

These patrons are a multitude as yet relatively little served by automated access. It will be by self-contained systems such as Laser Disc or CD/ROM that their needs will have to be addressed. Systems with monthly or even weekly cumulations sent by mail will sacrifice the instantaneous updating that VU/TEXT or DataTimes offer, but they will save communications and usage costs almost entirely. *InfoTrac*, in spite of its primitive searching capabilities, has been a tremendous success with the public. If one were to measure its value by dividing its yearly cost by the number of satisfied patrons who use it, one might reasonably decide that it is more cost effective than many a great reference book. Systems such as this are user friendly and directly available to library patrons, many of whom are familiar with personal computers.

REFERENCES

1. "Introduction" to volumes of *The Washington Post Index*.
2. K. D. Sell, "Checklist of Published Indexes to Current American Daily Newspapers," *RQ* 17, no. 1 (Fall 1977): 13-16.
3. Recent overviews include: Susan Spaeth Cherry, "Yesterday's News for Tomorrow: A Special Update on News Indexes, Indexing and Indexers," *American Libraries* 10, no. 10 (November 1979): 588-592; Stephen Smith, "Online News Retrieval Systems: Evaluations and Library Applications," *Reference Services Review* 10, no. 4 (Winter 1982): 47-60; Carol Tenopir, "Newspapers Online," *Library Journal* 109, no. 4 (March 1, 1984): 452-453.

4. A history of Bell & Howell's index production can be found in Russell H. Zesky, "Newspapers on Microfilm: History As It Was Happening (and Indexes to Help You Find Your Way)," *The Serials Librarian* 4, no. 4 (Summer 1980); 393-399.

5. For a review on the new *InfoTrac* installation at California State University at Chico, see Barbara Pease and William Post, "*InfoTrac:* A Review of an Optical Disc Based Public Index," *Serials Review* 11, no. 4 (Winter 1985): 57-61. At the University of Dayton, see Mary Ann Walker and Helen Westneat, "Using *InfoTrac* in an Academic Library," *Reference Services Review* 13, no. 4 (Winter 1985): 17-22. And at Colorado State University, see Douglas J. Ernest and Jennifer Monath, "User Reaction to a Computerized Periodical Index," *College & Research Libraries News* 47, no. 5 (May 1986): 315-318.

6. For a personal account of the development of *Information Bank* and some of the issues of the Mead Data Central contract, see Jeff Pemberton, "A Backward and Forward Look at *The New York Times Information Bank* — A Tale of Ironies Compounded . . . and an Analysis of the Mead Deal," *Online* 7, no. 4 (July 1983): 7-17.

7. For an introduction to VU/TEXT, see Donna Willman, "First Look: VU/TEXT Databases," *Online* 9, no. 2 (march 1985): 61-68. And for a review: Hunter McCleary, "VU-TEXT: Full-text Daily Newspaper Information and More," *Online* 9, no. 4 (July 1985): 87-94.

8. For a review of the two fulltext systems, see Reva Basch, "DataTimes. VU/TEXT," *RQ* 25, no. 4 (Summer 1986): 529-530.

Microcomputer Uses
in a State Newspaper Project

Rebecca M. Maier

SUMMARY. The United States Newspaper Project (USNP) is comprised of a number of state projects, each of which is responsible for identifying, locating, creating and making available catalog records for and preserving all extant newspapers published in that particular state. This paper presents a discussion of the most common uses of microcomputers in state newspaper projects. A summary of results from a survey made of all the state projects active in Phase II USNP activities as of May 1986 is presented with regard to the use in these projects of wordprocessing, database management, spreadsheet, electronic mail, and OCLC (Online Computer Library Center) software. From the results, it is clear that the advantages of using a microcomputer in a state newspaper project more than compensate for the initial costs. The number of uses for a microcomputer in all three phases of a newspaper project is almost unlimited. It can be advantageous during the initial planning and grant proposal writing phase, during the cataloging and collection of holdings phase, and during the microfilming preservation phase.

Given today's available software and computer technology, no state newspaper project should be without a microcomputer. Of course, instructions for the effective use of that microcomputer and software are also necessary. All state newspaper projects can benefit in terms of saving both money and time with a microcomputer. The number of newspaper titles and the number of years that newspapers have been published in a given state directly correlates to the time and money saved by the use of a microcomputer for that state's project. A state that was settled late may not have nearly as many titles to enter into a database as a state settled early, one, say, that has newspapers dating back to the 1700s. The uses of a microcomputer, then, would vary,

---

Rebecca M. Maier was employed for three years as the cataloging senior assistant for the Indiana Newspaper Project, c/o Indiana State Library, 140 N. Senate, Indianapolis, IN 46204. She holds a double BA degree in biology and psychology and is currently working on an MS degree in Industrial/Organizational Psychology.

depending upon the number of newspaper titles to be handled. Even the smallest state, however, could find many beneficial uses for a microcomputer during the various phases of its newspaper project. This article, although attempting to give examples of the most frequent uses made of microcomputers in a newspaper project, does not provide an exhaustive list. There are many more possibilities, some of which will be unique to each project's own special needs and will only be discovered once the projects are underway.

It is necessary to have access to an Online Computer Library Center (OCLC) terminal for entering the bibliographic and holdings information for newspapers into the USNP file. It is also very useful to have a microcomputer. These two items can be purchased as one unit called an M300 terminal, or they could be purchased separately as an OCLC terminal, such as the Beehive 105, and a standard microcomputer. The M300 has all of the necessary features for a newspaper project. The IBM personal computer (PC) is the basis of the M300. A comparable PC can be purchased for under $1,000. An M300 can be used as an OCLC terminal or as a microcomputer by switching the software used in it. Two separate pieces of equipment — a model 105 or 110 OCLC terminal and a stand-alone microcomputer — can of course be used simultaneously. Hookup costs, work space, access to other microcomputers, and the amount of time each system will be used should be considered before a purchase is made.

Maximum use of a newspaper project computer can be achieved by using three or four different types of software, besides the usual OCLC software. The first type of software is that used in a wordprocessing system. The second type is database management software for sorting, interfiling and collating. Another that would be useful is spreadsheet software; and a communications package is still another, this one recommended in the case of multi-sited rather than centrally located projects. Wordprocessing and database management software would cost between $50.00 and $700.00, depending on the brands and the capabilities desired. A spreadsheet such as Lotus 1,2,3 costs about $300.00. Training for personnel is an added expense, unless employees have had previous experience in the use of software. All of the needed items should be integrated into the proposed budget for a newspaper project.

Wordprocessing software is useful in dealing with many items, e.g., project correspondence; publicity such as articles or project description handouts; monthly reports and statistics; the developing and amending of forms; and the creating of lists of titles held in special collections, scattered issue microfilm reels, titles for each county in the state, etc. These are the major uses the Indiana Newspaper Project has made of its wordprocessing software during the project's Phase II or cataloging activity phase. Many of the other newspaper projects have made similar uses of their software as was learned in sending out a survey questionnaire (see Appendix 1).

There are also uses for a wordprocessing system in Phase I, the grant proposal phase of a project, and in Phase III, which involves the preservation of the newspapers by microfilming. Phase I can employ wordprocessing for writing the project proposal, since this allows for the easy adjusting of the proposal in the planning stages as new information is discovered or as adjustments occur in the proposed budget. The Phase III, preservation portion of the project, can likewise make use of the wordprocessing software for tasks such as creating title lists and for recording the location of materials to be collected in order to have available for microfilming the most complete run of any newspaper title in a county.

A database management software package for sorting/collating can be used in organizing the holdings of a particular site. For example, in the case of a list of older titles housed in a special collection and arranged alphabetically by city, a file of records might be made, each of which lists the paper's title, the city under which it is filed, the county of publication, and the years held in the storage area. The file could then be sorted to give a list by county of all information entered in the records. Such a rearrangement would of course be helpful when the file is alphabetical by city and the newspaper staff has found that working county by county is more logical and convenient. Thus, a list by city can be put in the database and a list by county can be taken out of it.

The file can also be sorted by any other field in the record. Another use would be to create a file of items held in newspaper collections that are omitted because they do not meet the project definition of a newspaper. Such a list would allow a newspaper section to know what titles were not cataloged and what holdings were not included during the project. This list could then be used in conjunction with the records entered into the OCLC database to achieve a complete survey of holdings. The list might also be used in cataloging at some later time the omitted titles.

Another possible use of a database management system is in the interfiling and sorting of information. It is very useful to be able to append records to existing files and then to have the system re-sort the files into the desired order. An example of such use might be to keep track of information about newspaper titles that have already been or are currently being microfilmed, and merging this information with information about titles still to be microfilmed. Another use of a database management system might be to keep track of repositories visited and their holdings, and the name of the person contacted there along with addresses and telephone numbers for each site. As new sites are visited, name/address information can be merged easily into the file. It is, moreover, very easy to produce labels for mass mailings from such a file.

A spreadsheet is useful in budget planning and in tracking of the budget during the course of the project. As expenses change, as OCLC costs increase, or as more monetary gifts are received, the spreadsheet can be easily updated. It can also be used in updating and totaling project statistics each month.

An electronic mail system allows for quick, detailed, communication among decentralized sites in a state project. It makes possible the easy transfer of information about titles cataloged, holdings identified, and so on. Such a system, moreover, simplifies coordination of microfilming efforts of Phase III. Each site can communicate holdings information and the physical condition of issues held. Electronic mail is not a necessity for all newspaper projects, because in some there is one major repository only. In such a case, the number of other repositories with which it would be necessary to communicate is likely to be small.

An essential piece of software for the M300 which is supplied by OCLC is a program called "keymap." This allows the M300 keyboard to become almost identical with the standard keyboard of the IBM personal computer. "Keymap 'remaps' the OCLC keyboard so that its IBM-mode key operations correspond to the engraved keycap labels."[1] Keymap must be loaded before using non-OCLC software that has been purchased for use with the PC mode of the M300 workstation.

A survey questionnaire (see Appendix 1) was sent to personnel at all fifteen newspaper projects who were working on the cataloging phase of the project in May, 1986. The questions were written to ascertain the computer and software needs of these projects. Fourteen of the fifteen projects returned the completed questionnaire (a 93.3% return rate). The project personnel were asked if they had an M300, OCLC terminal/personal computer; a separate microcomputer and an OCLC standard terminal; or simply an OCLC standard terminal without a personal computer. Eight of the fourteen, 57.1%, have the M300. The remaining six, 42.9%, do not have an M300. One of these six plans to purchase an M300, a second has a separate microcomputer, and a third has access to an off site microcomputer, which is used in conducting correspondence.

TABLE 1

TYPE OF COMPUTERS USED BY THE NEWSPAPER PROJECTS

	HAVE M300	PLAN TO BUY M300	HAVE SEPARATE MICROCOMPUTER	NO MICRO- COMPUTER	TOTAL
NUMBER OF NEWSPAPER PROJECTS	8	1	1	4	14

Nine of the fourteen, 64.3%, then, currently have a microcomputer. Of these nine, however, not all are fully using the capabilities of their microcomputers. Three of the eight, 37.5%, with the M300 combined OCLC terminal/PCs do not currently use the personal computer capability for anything, and listed no software as being purchased. Perhaps in these cases no money was budgeted for software. Another possible reason for not using the purchased microcomputer may be that the staff is not familiar with the capabilities of the computer and the advantages these provide. Two projects plan to purchase software but have not yet done so. Staff members at another project realize that they were underusing their M300. They did not use the personal computer capability at all, and had only defined two of their eight programmable function keys.

A programmable function key is a special key on the M300 terminal to which the user can assign a string of frequently typed characters and commands to save typing them often. In the Indiana newspaper project, all of the eight programmable function keys are defined, and several more could be defined, if more were available. As it is very easy to redefine a programmable function key for the M300, more time is saved by redefining it than by continuing to type an identical long field for every record. Some function keys that have been defined for the Indiana Project include one for the geographical code in the 752 MARC tag, "United States = b Indiana = c." This tag is automatically entered when the proper function key is depressed; and since it is used on the majority of records entered, a great deal of work is saved. Another key has been defined with the sign-on number and "send"; still another with "end" and "send."

Of the ten projects that have microcomputer capability (including the one with off site access), only six currently use it. All six, however, have wordprocessing software; and as some of the six have different wordprocessing systems at each of their sites, more than six wordprocessing software types are listed. The currently used software includes: Microsoft Word, Multimate, PC Write, Perfectwriter, PWP, Volkswriter, Wordperfect, Wordstar, and WP2 (for use on a Wang). Only one project noted dissatisfaction with its wordprocessing software. This was Perfectwriter, which the respondent said was hard to understand and use in the work the project was doing. Several projects wished they had more time to experiment with their software and so could become more proficient in its use.

Wordprocessing software is used more frequently than other software by four of the newspaper projects, but two projects did the majority of their work using a database management system. Four of the projects have database management software, with some sites within a state project having different brands. The ones used are: dBase III or dBase III+, Powerbase, and PC File III. All of the projects were satisfied with their database software.

Only two projects are currently using spreadsheet software. The software is Lotus 1, 2, 3 and Multiplan; and in both cases the use has to do with budgeting and statistics generation. One project plans to purchase spreadsheet software for keeping cataloging statistics and managing grant funds. The project that uses Multiplan was partially dissatisfied with it because "it does not hold unlimited titles" but it does allow easy sorting by the various columns in the spreadsheet.

Only one project is currently using an electronic mail system. This is PRLC/PALINET, which is the electronic mail system of the project's state library network. The project also has one site with Crosstalk software. The project does not use the electronic mail software nearly as much as it uses its wordprocessing or database management system, but feels that the electronic mail capability may become more useful in the third phase of the project, that during which microfilming is undertaken while cataloging and holdings records are still being created, as at that point coordinating the various procedures involved will be difficult. Five of the eight projects with an M300 are using the IBM PC attributes of the system. Additionally, two projects have other sites, one with a Wang computer, and the other with a COMPAQ computer. Another project has a Burroughs B-20 computer.

Even though the advantages far outweigh them, there are a few disadvantages in using a computer as the repository for all the data. A power failure may lead to many lost hours of work. The data that had been entered all afternoon may be lost in a split second by the power's going out. Another way in which data can be lost is in failure to follow assiduously the software instructions when exiting the system. Data entered is lost when the computer is turned off without properly saving the files. Usually, the lesson is well remembered after one such mishap, as reentering the data is a painstaking process. Frequent datasaving while working on a file may decrease the risks involved. Another problem is that a diskette with all the data files on it may wear out, but if a backup diskette is made often enough, the seriousness of this problem is reduced. The only data lost in such a case is that entered since the last backup diskette was made. If, however, the backup diskette is not checked to make sure the data was copied onto it correctly, all the data could again be lost. The moral is that backup diskettes should be made often, and checked to ensure that they work. Producing paper printouts is also a good idea. When someone is using the M300 in the OCLC mode, it is not then necessary to interrupt the user to look at the data files in the personal computer, since the printout is available.

One obvious disadvantage of a microcomputer is its high cost. The price of the computer itself, the software, the cables, the computer paper, diskettes, and printer must all be considered. It might be supposed that a typewriter, a bottle of liquid correcting fluid, typing paper, and some extra hours of employee time would easily replace a computer. The extra employee hours, however, would alone cost more than do the computer and the equipment that goes with it. At the Indiana Newspaper Project many staff hours were spent coordinating information about titles held in several locations in the Indiana State Library and the Indiana Historical Society. The earliest issue in each case had to be found for cataloging purposes, and so a list was made of holdings in all locations. This task, just about impossible if it had to be carried out manually, was accomplished, using a computer, with relative ease. When an OCLC terminal must be purchased anyway, the extra money should be spent to buy an M300 terminal unless a personal computer is already available. If a personal computer is going to be used in the third phase of the project, it makes sense to purchase it for use in the other phases of the project, too, especially if these will all be carried out in the same location, where presumably the computer can be shared. As suggested earlier, one advantage of having a separate microcomputer and an OCLC terminal in place of the M300 is that this allows two people to work simultaneously on computer tasks. The advantage here is not of course all that great in the case of a small newspaper project, if time on the personal computer can be limited to when OCLC is not needed.

There is a definite need for microcomputers and software suited to the budgets and needs of the national newspaper projects. Many of the states that have not begun their projects should attempt now to budget the money necessary for the computer, software, printer, and training for their project. The responses to the survey questionnaire might serve as a list of the software needs and uses for future newspaper projects. It can be hoped that the National Endowment for the Humanities (NEH), which sponsors the United States Newspaper Project, will encourage the individual states to submit proposals which include in their budgets money for a computer and software. NEH might also encourage, perhaps by means of a newsletter or an electronic mail system, the sharing among the various state newspaper projects of information about computer software uses and problems. Good communication is an important aspect of the United States Newspaper Project, and computers are an important topic about which information should be shared. The possible uses of computers in a state project are only limited by the user's imagination.

REFERENCE NOTE

1. *OCLC M300 Guide to Operations*, 3rd ed, OCLC Online Computer Library Center, Inc., 1984, p. 5:22.

APPENDIX 1

QUESTIONNAIRE ON THE USE OF MICROCOMPUTERS IN NEWSPAPER PROJECTS
PLEASE USE THE BACK OF THE PAGE IF MORE SPACE IS NEEDED.

1. Does your newspaper project use a M300 OCLC terminal/personal computer?

                              Yes   No

   If yes, skip to question 4b.

2. If no, do you have access to another microcomputer?

                              Yes   No

   If you answered "No" to both of the above questions, complete question 3 and you are done.

   If you answered "Yes," skip to question 4.

3. Are you currently trying to purchase or gain access to a microcomputer? If yes, please cite what would be the major utilization of that computer?

                              Yes   No

4. What type of microcomputers do you use and what software programs are used for the newspaper project work ?

   a. Type of computer:

   b. Software programs--please specify (e.g., Wordstar, Lotus 1,2,3, dBase II or III, etc.)

APPENDIX I (continued)

5. Briefly state what products are produced by each software package. For example,

       Wordstar: making mailing labels, monthly statistic reports
       dBase III: making lists of the newspaper titles held in special collections.
       PC write: general correspondence and publicity about the project.

   Also indicate what software is used most frequently, for example 90% of our personal computer work is done in Wordstar.

6. Are you satisfied with your present software? Why or why not?
       Yes   No

The Effects of Emerging Technologies on Newspaper Storage and Retrieval

J. J. Hayden III

SUMMARY. This paper seeks to explore the impact that using microcomputer-based optical disc storage systems has on newspaper archival storage. An attempt is made to define methods that can be used to categorize the types of data found on the pages of newspapers, show how that information can be stored in a digital format, and determine the quantity of computer storage media required. The characteristics of the computer hardware, software, and storage structures are also examined. The paper also explores some ramifications of using existing technology to capture newspapers in machine-readable form, as well as some of the benefits and problems that may occur with use of the new technologies.

How is emerging technology likely to affect the archival storage of and access to newspapers? What are some of the advantages and disadvantages of the new technologies?

In 1986 the dominant archival storage technology for newspapers is based on photographic film as the primary storage media. Yet this media has not been proven to be as permanent as some of the newspapers that it is used to "preserve." The storage, retrieval and preservation of film media presents a much smaller problem than does working with the original documents; but locating particular information, such as a specific issue of a newspaper, from one or a collection of newspapers housed on film media can be a time-consuming process. The storage of the film media also presents problems of preservation and access. For several years the digital computer has been used to assist in indexing and retrieving documents on film media,[1] but these docu-

---

J. J. Hayden is Special Projects Coordinator at the Southeastern Library Network, in Atlanta, Georgia. He holds a BS from the University of Southern Mississippi in Computer Science and Statistics. He has a wide range of computer experience and for the last six years has been actively involved in utilizing the microcomputer and other new technology to solve information systems problems.

ment control systems are very expensive and subject to problems with the hardware used for storage and retrieval.

If one were to examine the products offered by vendors in a related field, information retrieval, the obvious trend is toward the use of microcomputers and optical disc technology. The development of microprocessors such as the IBM AT and the Commodore Amiga has produced equipment that will fit on a desk top, yet has the speed and processing power of mainframe computers. Along with this increased power to manipulate data has come a new type of storage media, the optical disc, which has the capacity to store one billion, two hundred million characters (1,200,000,000 or 1.2 gigabytes) on a single 12-inch disc. The optical disc has the storage space for very large databases and the microminiaturized mainframe has the magnitude of computing power needed to manipulate large text databases. This combination of technologies holds a great deal of promise for the archival storage of newspapers.[2] There are some difficulties, however, that must be addressed before computer optical disc systems will replace the existing film based systems.

There are two major types of optical discs: non-erasable and erasable. All optical discs use some type of laser to record information on the disc. The laser is used to place digital data (specifically 1's and 0's) on the media. In the case of the non-erasable optical disc, the laser actually changes the surface of the disc by forming a bubble or melting a pit along a circular track on it. This physical change of the surface of the medium has led to the estimate of a ten-year lifespan for data stored on optical discs. This ten-year estimate is based on accelerated life testing, a method of observing the results of a rigorous test and estimating the time required to produce similar results in normal use.[3] The conservative nature of this estimate can be understood when one considers that the layer of the media that holds the bubble or pit is completely encapsulated so that the data representing marks are not exposed to wear. Additionally, the technique to read the recorded data uses a beam of light from a low power laser to detect the presence or absence of holes or pits; this means that only photons touch the data holding surface of the disc. The question of data lifespan, then, can be loosely described as the length of time it takes the photons to fill the hole, or burst the "plastic" bubble.

The optical disc comes in three diameters: 3 1/2, 5 1/4, and 12 inches. The storage capacity of the three is respectively, 50, 600, and 1,200 megabytes. The only type of optical disc, compact disc Read Only Memory (CD-ROM) available on the market in mid-1986 is of the non-erasable sort. There is a writable optical disc, called a write once read mostly (WORM) drive, but the data on this type of device is not erasable. With the WORM configuration, when data on the disc is superseded as information is written on the disc, the old data is marked as deleted, but the space on the surface of the media is not reusable. The disc will have to be replaced or used in read only mode when the space available on which to write is used up. The Verbatim Corporation exhibited an erasable thermo-megnato-optical disc at the 1985 National Computer Conference. The projection is that a 50 megabyte, 3 1/2 inch disc will be on the market by 1988. This technology uses a laser to heat a small area of the disc as a strong magnetic field is applied, a combination that causes the magnetic orientation of the medium to change. The magnetic areas in the disc can be read much as traditional magnetic media are read, and the data on the disc can be erased and then rewritten. The combination of a strong magnetic field and a laser needed to record data on the disc means that this media is unlikely to be affected by x-ray machines, electric motors, and other common hazards that would be deadly when transporting traditional magnetic media. Most observers indicate, however, that there is a place in the future for existing magnetic media and for both types of optical discs. The basic requirements have not changed: more capacity for data, faster rates of data transfer, and longevity of data retention. All three of these parameters seem to be part of the future of optical disc technology.

Newspapers are one of the few information sources whose contents, once issued, are truly static. This characteristic allows for the use of non-erasable optical disc technology as the medium for archival storage of newspapers. The primary reason for using optical disc technology to store newspapers and their indexes is the requirement for large amounts of space. Computers are adept at storing and retrieving character data, that is letters, numbers, and any other ASCII (American Standard Code for Information Interchange) element. One ASCII character occupies one byte of storage. The following table (Table 1) shows the amount of storage provided by magnetic and optical media used on existing computer systems.

TABLE 1

Type of media	Storage in bytes
Removable magnetic disc	114,000 to 40,000,000
Non-removable magnetic disc	10,000,000 to 1,000,000,000
Optical disc	600,000,000 to 1,200,000,000

The following example illustrates the space required to store a newspaper. If a newspaper prints an *average* of 17.5 characters per inch in six, 2 inch wide columns that are 22 inches long, then there would be 4,620 characters per page. This means that a 12 inch optical disc with 1.2 gigabyte capacity could hold 260,000,000 pages of newsprint. But newspapers are not just text, there is much in each issue of a newspaper that is graphic information, that is titles, pictures and drawings in color, black, white, and shades of gray. The space required to store graphic data is considerably greater than that for text. A printed picture is made up of picture elements called "pels" in print shop jargon or "pixels" in computerese. The smaller the picture element, the better the appearance of the picture. Newspapers use densities of from 3600 to 57,600 pels per square inch. The most common densities are 3600, and 14,400 pels/square inch. Table 2 shows the requirements for storing some types of pictures at the lowest density.

TABLE 2

Storage of graphic data at 3600 pels/inch^2

Type of graphic	Basic storage unit	Bytes per inch^2
Black and white	.8 pels/byte	450
Gray scale of 16 shades from black to white	.2 pels/byte	1800
Color: 16 colors with 16 intensity levels	.1 pel/byte	3600

This implies that a full page, 13 by 22 inch picture of 286 square inches would require from 128,700 to 1,029,600 bytes of storage using the minimum resolution of 60 × 60 pels/inch. Thus, if newspapers with color pictures or drawings were simply recorded with a color video camera or optical scanner at the density indicated above, fewer than 1.2 million pages of newsprint as compared to 260 million for text alone, could be stored on a 12 inch optical disc. Most scanners used to convert pictures or drawings into digital data scan at rates of from 200 to 400 pixels per linear inch, or 40,000 to 160,000 pixels per square inch. This means that a 16 color/intensity recording method would record a full page in 11,440,000 to 45,760,000 bytes of space or approximately 104 to 26 pages respectively per 12 inch optical disc.[4] These figures seem to point out that the degree of detail in current scanning methods is considerably greater than necessary, especially when the pels/inch of the original newsprint is compared to the pixels/inch of the digitized image. The manufacturers of scanning equipment have attempted to ensure that the detailed engineering drawings or fine print of technical journals can be accurately stored in a computer file and reproduced on a high resolution monitor or a laser printer. Newspapers would appear to be at the other end of the spectrum. A resolution of 100 by 100 or 10,000 pixels per square inch would be 2.7 times the 3,600 pels per square inch resolution of most newspaper graphics. At the 10,000 pixels per square inch density, 2,860,000 bytes are required to store full page color graphics or approximately 419 full page pictures could be stored on a 12 inch optical disc. The best compromise for storing newsprint in digital form would seem to be a combination of both text and picture formats, in which the pictures are broken down into black and white, gray scale, and color. The capability to store information in both digital (1's and 0's) and analog (video tape) formats is found in CD-I, or compact disc-interactive, optical disc media.[5] This implies not only that newspaper data can be stored in different formats (e.g., black and white, shades of gray, and color) but also that in some types of pictures, such as full page advertisements, video "pictures" in the format used for home TVs can be stored on the disc. Table 3 shows the amount of newsprint, in square inches, found in representative samples from the first section of several current newspapers.

TABLE 3

Area in Square Inches Occupied by:

Newspaper	# Pages	Text	B.&W.	Gray Scale	Color
Wall Street Journal	32	1668	4182	2435	0
U.S.A. Today	14	769	1442	250	775
Indianapolis Star	30	1112	3609	2912	54
Atlanta Journal Constitution (Sunday ed.)	22	1264	2848	3324	70

This proliferation of types of optical media and formats of data on them could inhibit manufacturers and system integrators from selecting optical disc media as a storage device because of the lack of any standards. Members of the optical disc industry are, however, addressing this problem, and have produced a standard for optical media. Called the "High Sierra Group" — for the location of the first meeting, an hotel at Lake Tahoe — and made up of manufacturers, system integrators, and other interested parties, this group has put forth a set of standards defining types of optical disc that can be used with computer systems.[6] The optical disc will become an accepted part of computer systems only if standards exist to ensure that media, and devices are transportable and interchangeable from system to system.

The procedures used to record or digitize printed material for storage in computer systems is not very different from the procedures used with film media. Every sheet of printed material must be scanned using equipment similar to that used for microfilm. The process of recording large numbers of current newspapers is of course cumbersome, and would be greatly simplified if the computer systems used to compose and typeset newspapers could provide machine-readable output media. The tapes or discs from the newspaper system could then be used to place the data onto optical discs. Several larger newspapers daily convert each edition of their newspapers into digital format for transmission to regional publishing sites. The system could easily place this electronic newspaper on an optical disc as it goes to press.

Perhaps the most interesting aspect of storing large text databases on optical disc systems is that a variety of indices could be created from the text and stored on the *same* media as the data. Such indices would provide multiple points of access to the information stored on the disc. In large-scale data processing systems, the creation and placement of indices on the same discs or media as the data is already common practice. The implication for newspapers seems obvious. A large volume, low price storage medium, such as the optical disc, would provide room for a large mass of source data and still leave room for the indexes needed to access the data. For example, if a system were to allocate 50 bytes of storage per keyword and maintained a thesaurus of 10,000 entries this would occupy 500,000 bytes of space. If there were an average of 10 references in the data file for each keyword, this would use 5,000,000 bytes of storage. For a device that can store 1,200,000,000 bytes, 36 thesaurus/cross-reference files, of 5 megabytes each, could be placed on the disc and still leave 1 gigabyte of storage space. This implies that there would be room to index the pictures, advertisements, and even the comics as well as the text. Optical disc technology would seem to provide solutions to some of the problems connected with the storage and retrieval of large amounts of data, and especially multi-format data (i.e., text, and pictures). The most significant of these problems is the need to handle tremendous volumes of data requiring large amounts of storage space, as well as additional space for the auxiliary files used in retrieving the data.

Given the fact that it is feasible to store large amounts of source data and their associated indexes on optical discs, the question of actual data retrieval still remains. Despite the best attempts of providers of information retrieval systems to produce auxiliary files so that data is retrievable in many ways, there is always the need to search text one letter, word, or phrase at a time. If exact, character-by-character matches are the only type required, a digital computer can perform the search task, although searching a large amount of text can take a long time. But what of inexact matches? That is, suppose that the search system were asked to return all occurrences where "optical disc" was within 50 characters of the word "computer." This type of proximity search can take even more computer power and time than exact character matches. It is significant to note that the database systems that are the fastest at fetching data tend to use this inexact match procedure. At the National Computer Conference in July, 1985, a company called Proximity Technology exhibited a product that implements proximity searches at the hardware level. This product takes the process of searching away from the main processor and does the work on a printed circuit board that plugs into an IBM-PC.[7] A table shows the closeness of fit, expressed as a percentage of the data found in the database to the requested data. The retrieval software can then decide which if any of the data has met the search requirements. For very large databases, where nonexact matches are needed, this helping hand is just what the microcomputer needs.

The merging of information retrieval and artificial intelligence software systems seems to be taking place on the optical disc.[8] The basic idea is to have the retrieval system assist the user in searching the database. As a user goes through the process of developing and refining a search, for example, specifying sets and subsets by ANDing, ORing, and NOTing search results, the search system can recognize and record search patterns. Over time the search system builds a profile of the user's search requests and consults the profile to assist in retrieving information. The storage requirements for recording the history of use of a search system by multiple users, as well as for that of the auxiliary index files created by analysis of the search histories could easily be found in writable or erasable optical disc technology.

Current trends strongly suggest that machine-readable format storage systems are part of the future of document storage. The fact that newspapers are one of the most voluminous forms of documents and that, once issued, they do not change, makes them an especially appropriate target for storage on optical disc read only memory. The associated indexes, search history files, thesauri, and other auxiliary files use a significant amount of storage space, but unlike the newspapers themselves, these do change. Erasable/rewritable storage must, then, be part of the system. Additionally, specialized hardware components must be used to assist the processor in locating data not found by using existing indices.

The large volume of storage space made available by optical disc technology, the power of microprocessors and specialized search hardware, and advances in information retrieval techniques will provide tools to mine the information resources provided by newspaper archives.

REFERENCES

1. R. J. Kalthoff. "Document-Based Optical Mass Memories?" *Information Management*, Vol. 18, No. 8 September 1985.
2. C. A. Lynch and E. B. Brownrigg. "Library Applications of Electronic Imaging Technology," *Information Technology and Libraries* Vol. 5, No. 2.
3. A. S. Hoagland. "Information Storage Technology: A Look at the Future," *Computer*, Vol. 18, No. 7.
4. J. P. McNaul. "Image Capture and Processing for CD ROM," *CD Rom the New Papyrus*, Microsoft Press, 1986.
5. W. W. Conhaim. "Videotext 86: Videotext Applications Outlive Industry Event," *Information Today*, Vol. 3, No. 6, June 1986.
6. D. Gabel. "Optical Disk Storage," Supplement to *PC Week* Section 2, Vol. 3, No. 24, June 17, 1986.
7. *PF474 Product Data Book*, Proximity Technology Inc., 1984.
8. E. A. Fox. "Information Retrieval: Research into New Capabilities," *CD ROM the New Papyrus*, Microsoft Press, 1986.

Index

Abstracting, of newspaper articles, 73,75, 76-78
Accession procedures, for newspapers, 54-56
Acquisition, of newspapers, 67,95
Acta Diurna Populi Romani, 125
Adoption notices, as genealogical research source, 50
Air Force Times, 122
ALA Glossary of Library and Information Science, newspaper definition, 94
American Antiquarian Society, 8,16,18
American Banner, 100
American Council of Learned Societies, 4
American National Standard for Serial Holdings Statements, 9
American Newspaper Directory, 15
American Newspapers, 1821-1936 (Gregory), 2,3-4,52
Amsterdam News, index, 134
Anglo-American Cataloging Rules (AACR) 2
 title variations, 23-24,26,27
 uniform titles, 24-25,26,27
 United States Newspaper Program applications, 5-7
Army Times, 122,123
Army Times Publishing Company, 122
Army-Navy Journal, 123,124
Army-Navy Register, 124
Association of Research Libraries, Foreign Newspaper Microfilm Project (FNMP), 65,69
Atex editorial front-end system, 80-81,91

Balch Institute, 69
Baltimore News-American, 122
Bell & Howell, newspaper indexes, 134-135, 139-140
Belmont Conference, 3
Bigelow, Donald, N., 123
Biloxi Seashore Sentinel, 105
Birth notices, as genealogical research source, 50
Brazil Times, 119

BRS, 136
Burnside, Ambrose, 123
Burnside Committee, 123-124

Canada, Decentralized Program for Canadian Newspaper Preservation and Access, 126-127
Carnegie Foundation, 5
Cataloging, of newspapers, 94
 by Center for Research Libraries, 67-69
 by Indiana Newspaper Project, 51-52
 International Guidelines for the Cataloging of Newspapers, 128-129
 on microfilm, 6-7
 uniform titles, 21-27
  definition, 24-25
  problem regarding, 21-24
  proposal regarding, 25-26
  proposed record, 26-27
 by United States Newspaper Program, 5-7, 8,9,23-27,68-69
Center for Research Libraries (CRL), newspaper collections, 63-70
 cataloging, 67-69
 foreign newspapers, 65,67
 interlibrary loan, 66
 microfilming, 69-70
 preservation, 69-70
 technical processing, 66-69
 United States Newspaper Program participation, 8,68-69
 U.S. ethnic newspapers, 64-65,70
 U.S. general circulation newspapers, 64
Chicago Tribune, 122
Christian Science Monitor, index, 134,136, 138
Church, Frederick, 123
Church, William C., 123
Clipping file, 73-79
 abstracting procedures, 73,75,76-78
 filing procedures, 75,79
 indexing procedures, 73,74,75,83-90
 microfilming procedures, 79

161

Common Cause Magazine, 122
CONSER Program, United States Newspaper Program and, 4-5,6,8,9,68
Cook, Kenneth, 115,116
Council on Library Resources, 3
Current News, 121-122

Daily Oklahoman, 139
Database management, 144,145-146
DataTek Corporation, 139
DataTimes, 139
Deaccession procedures, for newspapers, 52-53,59-62
Death certificates, as genealogical research source, 50
Decentralized Program for Canadian Newspaper Preservation and Access, 126-127
Desktop publishing, 10
DIALOG, 81,136
Directory of Newspapers and Periodicals, 15
Display, of newspapers, 50-51
Dow Jones database, 81

Editorials on File, 135
Electronic files, 80-81,82
Electronic mail, 146,148

Facts on File, 135
Facts on File News Digest, 135
Farqurean, Lightfoot B., 116
Files, in newspaper reference library
  electronic, 80-81,82
  filing procedures, 75,79
  vertical, 80
Filing procedures, in newspaper reference library, 75,79
Florida Union List of Serials, 6n.
Foreign Newspaper Microfilm Project (FNMP), 65,69

Genealogical columns, 114-117
Genealogical Helper, 116
Genealogical research, newspapers as sources in, 50,109-120
  genealogical columns, 114-117
  librarians and, 113,116-118
  obituaries, 110-113
  personal columns, 117
Gutgesell, Stephen, 14

Handsboro Democrat, 101
Harriman, Robert, 129

Hazen, William B., 121,123,124
Hill, Frank P., 29,30
Historical research, newspapers as sources in, 1,50-51. *See also* Genealogical research, newspapers as sources in
  on microfilm, 99-107
History and Bibliography of American Newspapers, 1690-1820 (Brigham), 2,15
Höfig, Willi, 128

Immigration History Research Center, 69
IMS Directory of Publications, 52
Indexes, to newspapers, 2,10,95-96,133-141
  Amsterdam News, 134
  Bell & Howell's, 134-135,139-140
  Christian Science Monitor, 134,136,138
  computerized indexing and, 133-134,139
  DataTimes, 139
  Editorials on File, 135
  Facts on File, 135
  Facts on File News Digest, 135
  first, 133
  in Indiana State Library Newspaper Section, 52
  Info Globe, 139
  InfoTrac, 136-137,140
  Keesing's Contemporary Archives, 135
  local, 133
  Los Angeles Times, 136,138
  machine-readable, 134,135,136-139,140
  on microfilm, 134,136
  National Newspaper Index, 136,139
  NDEX, 135
  NewSearch, 136
  New York Times, 2,133,134,135,136,137, 138-139
    as subject heading source, 73
  New York Times Information Bank, 138
  NewsBank, 135,137
  NewsBank Electronic Index, 135,137
  for newspaper reference library clipping file, 73,74,75,83-90
  NEXIS, 138-139
  on optical disc, 136-137,158,159
  printed, 134-136,137,139-140
  techniques, 96
  USA Today, 134
  VU/TEXT, 139,140
  Wall Street Journal, 2,135,136,137
  Washington Post, 136,138
Indiana Gazette, 44
Indiana Historical Society

Indiana Newspaper Bibliography and, 13, 19
newspaper collection, 51
Newspaper Microfilm Project, 19,37-41, 46,49
  cost, 40
  objectives, 38
  procedures, 38-40
  repository sources, 40-41
Indiana Newspaper Bibliography, 13-20,25
  bibliographic sources, 15-17
  format, 17-19
  Indiana Historical Society and, 13,19
  microfilm copies, 18
  newspapers' political affiliations, 18-19,20
  non-extant titles, 15-16
  repository questionnaire, 16-17
  research aids, 19
Indiana Newspaper Bibliography (Miller), 51
Indiana Newspaper Project, 49,51-52
Indiana State Library, Newspaper Section, 43-62
  access, 51-52
  accession procedures, 54-56
  cataloging, 52-53
  collection policy, 44-47
  deaccession procedures, 52-53,59-62
  holdings, 44
  indexing, 52
  interlibrary loan, 49
  microfilm collection, 44,45,46,47
  preservation, 47-49
  preservation survey, 31-33,35-36
  reference services, 49-51,52
  storage, 48,49
  subscriptions, 45-46
Indianapolis News, The, 50,72,73,75,76-78, 79,80,81
Indianapolis Newspaper Inc. Library, 71-91
  book collection, 80
  clipping file, 73-79
    abstracting procedures, 73,75,76-78
    filing procedures, 75,79
    indexing procedures, 73,74,75,83-90
    microfilming procedures, 79
  electronic files, 80-81,82
  information retrieval services, 81,90-91
  newspaper collection, 80
  periodicals collection, 80
  picture files, 79-80,90
  purpose, 71-72
  reference services, 81-90

velox files, 79,80,90
vertical files, 80
Indianapolis Star, The, 51,72,73,75,76-78, 79,80,81
Info Globe, 139
Information retrieval
  in newspaper reference library, 81,90-91
  on optical disc, 158-160
InfoTrac, 136-137,140
Interlibrary loan, of newspapers
  by Center for Research Libraries, 66
  on microfilm, 49
International activities, in newspaper librarianship, 125-131
  Decentralized Program for Canadian Newspaper Preservation and Access, 126-127
  International Federation of Library Associations and Institutions (IFLA), Working Group on Newspapers, 127-130
  International Guidelines for the Cataloging of Newspapers, 128-129
  international standardization, 129-130
  international symposium, 130
  Newspaper Conservation Project, 129
  Survey of National Newspaper Collections, 128
International Guidelines for the Cataloging of Newspapers, 128-129

Jane's Defense Weekly, 124
Joint Committee of Bibliographical Services to History, 3
Journal of the Armed Forces, 124
Journal of the Armed Forces International, 124

Kansas State Historical Society, 8
Keesing's Contemporary Archives, 135
Komorous, Hana, 129

Laser disc. *See* Optical disc
Library Literature, 97
Library of Congress (LC)
  newspaper definition, 6,14,44
  newspaper microfilming activities, 65,69
  United States Newspaper Program and, 3, 4,5-6,7,8,68,69
Library schools, newspaper librarianship courses, 30,34-35,93-97
Livingston, Larry G., 5
Los Angeles Times, index, 136,138

MacNamara, Robert, 122
Mannerheim, Johan, 128
MARC format, 4,5,9,68
Marriage certificates, as genealogical research source, 50
Masthead title changes, 2,67
  uniform titles and, 21-27
Metzger, Joyce Owen, 114
Microcomputers
  optical disc newspaper storage applications, 154-160
    data retrieval process, 158-160
    disc types, 154-155
    indexes, 158,159
    procedures, 157-158
    standards, 157
    storage capacity, 155-157
  state newspaper projects applications, 143-151
    cost, 143,144,149
    database management, 144,145-146
    disadvantages, 148-149
    electronic mail, 146,148
    hardware, 144,146-147,148-149,150
    OCLC and, 144,146
    software, 144-146,147-148,149,150-151
    spreadsheet, 144,146,148
    wordprocessing, 144-145,147-148,150, 151
Microfilm, newspapers on, 94
  cataloging of, 6-7
  Center for Research Libraries collections, 64,65-66,67,69-70
  deterioration, 31,34
  ethnic newspapers, 70
  foreign newspapers, 65,67
  as historical research source, 99-107
  indexes to, 134,136
  Indiana State Library Newspaper Section Survey, 32-34
  interlibrary loan, 49
  inventories, 34
  storage, 32,33,49
Microfilming, of newspapers, 2,94
  by Center for Research Libraries, 69-70
  cost, 34
  by Decentralized Program for Canadian Newspaper Preservation and Access, 126-127
  by Indiana Historical Society Newspaper Microfilm Project, 19,37-41,46,49
    cost, 40
    objectives, 38
    procedures, 38-40
    repository sources, 40-41
  by International Federation of Library Associations and Institutions Newspaper Conservation Project, 129
  by Library of Congress, 65,69
  for newspaper reference library clipping file, 79
  quality control methods, 30-31,33-34
  standards, 130
  by United States Newspaper Program, 8
Microfilming of Newspapers on 35mm Unperforated Microfilm for Archival Purposes, 130
Midwest Inter-Library Center, 63
Military Review, 124
Minnesota Union List of Serials, 6n.
Mississippi Gulf Coast: Portrait of a People (Sullivan), 105-107
Montana, United States Newspaper Program bibliographic grant, 8
Morgue, 71. See also Newspaper reference library

National Endowment for the Humanities (NEH)
  Indiana Newspaper Bibliography and, 14
  United States Newspaper Project and, 3,4, 7,8,9,68,150
National Library of Canada, Decentralized Program for Canadian Newspaper Preservation and Access, 126-127
National Newspaper Index, 136,139
Navy Times, 122
NDEX, 135
New Orleans Daily Cresent, 99-100,101-103
New Orleans Daily Delta, 100,103-104,105
New Orleans Daily Picayune, 104-105
New York Historical Society, 8
New York Public Library, newspaper microfilming activities, 69
New York Times, 122
  as genealogical research source, 119-120
  index, 2,133,134,135,136,137,138-139
  as subject heading source, 73
New York Times Information Bank, 138
News and Record, 114-115
NewsBank, 135,137
NewsBank Electronic Index, 135,137
NewSearch, 136
Newspaper(s). See also names of individual newspapers

acquisition, 67,95
bibliographic control, 2. *See also*
    Cataloging, of newspapers
binding, 48
definitions, 94
    International Federation of Library
        Associations and Institutions, 130
    Library of Congress, 6,14,44
    standards for, 130
display of, 50-51
ethnic, 64-65,70
foreign
    acquisition, 67
    backfiles, 63-64
    Center for Research Libraries collection, 65,67
    on microfilm, 65,67
as genealogical research source, 50, 109-120
    genealogical columns, 114-117
    librarians and, 113,116-118
    obituaries, 50,110-113
    personal columns, 117
handling, 1-2
historical background, 125
as historical research source, 1
    as exhibits, 50-51
    on microfilm, 99-107
indexes/indexing. *See* Indexes, to newspapers
machine-readable form, 94
    online searching of, 96
masthead title changes, 2,67
    uniform titles and, 21-27
on microfilm. *See* Microfilm, newspapers on
microfilming. *See* Microfilming, of newspapers
military, 121-124
non-extant titles, 10,15-16
paper types, 31-32,33,47-48,69
photocopying of, 51
preservation. *See* Preservation, of newspapers
storage. *See* Storage, of newspapers
symposium, 130
Newspaper Cataloging Manual, 5-7,24,68
Newspaper Conservation Project, 129
Newspaper librarianship, education for, 30, 34-35,93-97
Newspaper reference library, 71-91
    book collection, 80

clipping file, 73-79
    abstracting procedures, 73,75,76-78
    filing procedures, 75,79
    indexing procedures, 73,74,75,83-90
    microfilming procedures, 79
electronic files, 80-81,82
information retrieval services, 81,90-91
newspaper collection, 80
periodicals collection, 80
picture files, 79,80,90
purpose, 71-72
reference services, 81-90
    access, 83,90
    public service, 83
velox files, 79,80,90
vertical file, 80
Newspapers in Microform: United States, 2, 15,52
NEXIS, 81,138-139

Obituaries, as genealogical research source, 50,110-113
Ocean Springs Naiad, 104-105
OCLC
    Indiana Newspaper Project and, 49,51
    United States Newspaper Program and, 4, 5,8,9,68,69
    microcomputer use in, 144,145,146,147
Online Computer Library Center. *See* OCLC
Optical disc
    newspaper indexes on, 136-137,140,158, 159
    newspaper storage on, 34,154-160
        data retrieval process, 158-160
        disc types, 154-155
        indexes, 158,159
        procedures, 157-158
        standards, 157
        storage capacity, 155-157
ORBIT, 135
Organization of American Historians (OAH)
    Indiana Newspaper Bibliography and, 14
    United States Newspaper Program and, 3-4,5

Palmer's Index to the Times Newspaper, 133
Parameters: Journal of the U.S. Army War College, 124
Periodicals collection, in newspaper reference library, 80
Personal columns, as genealogical research source, 117
Photocopying, of newspapers, 51

Picture files, in newspaper reference library, 79-80,90
Pittsburgh Union List of Serials, 6n.
Preservation, of newspapers, 29-36. *See also* Microfilm, newspapers on; Microfilming, of newspapers; Storage, of newspapers
　by Center for Research Libraries, 69-70
　by Indiana State Library Newspaper Section, 47-49
　Indiana State Library Newspaper Section survey, 31-32,35-36
　international efforts, 125-131
　　Decentralized Program for Canadian Newspaper Preservation and Access, 126-127
　　International Federation of Library Associations and Institutions (IFLA), Working Group on Newspapers, 129
　preservation copies, 29
　training for, 30,95
Price, Mary S., 129
Publick Occurencies, 125

Reference services
　of Indiana State Library Newspaper Section, 49-51,52
　in newspaper reference library, 81-90
Relacíon del Terremoto de Guatemala, 125
St. Louis Post-Dispatch, 122
Schroder, Al, 14
Sears List of Subject Headings, 73
Sherman, William Tecumseh, 123
Snider, Sarah Shake, 116
Source: A Guidebook of American Genealogy, The (Eakle and Cerny, eds.), 120
Special Libraries Association, Newspaper Division, 97
Spreadsheets, 144,146,148
Standards, international
　for microfilm, 129-130
　for newspaper definitions, 130
State Historical Society of Wisconsin, 8
Stellhorn, Paul, 14
Stevens, M. James, 106-107
Storage, of newspapers, 2,3,29
　by Indiana State Library Newspaper Section, 48,49
　Indiana State Library Newspaper Section survey of, 32,35,36
　on microfilm, 32,33,49
　　standards, 129-130

　on optical disc, 34,154-160
　　data retrieval process, 158-160
　　disc types, 154-155
　　indexes, 158,159
　　procedures, 157-158
　　standards, 157
　　storage capacity, 155-157
　on photographic film, 153
Sullivan Union, 112-113
Survey of National Newspaper Collections, 128
Sydney Gazette, 125
Symposium, on newspapers, 130
Szucs, Loretto Dennis, 120

Technical processing, of newspapers, 66-69. *See also* Cataloging, of newspapers; Preservation, of newspapers; Storage, of newspapers
Time, 122
Ti-pao, 125
Toronto Globe and Mail, 139

Uniform titles, of newspapers, 21-27
　definition, 24-25
　problem regarding, 21-24
　proposal regarding, 25-26
　proposed record, 26-27
Union lists, of newspapers, 2,6n.
　newspaper cataloging and, 7,8
　United States Newspaper Program and, 7-8,69
United States News and World Report, 122
United States Newspaper Program (USNP), 3-10
　bibliographic grants, 8
　cataloging
　　Anglo-American Cataloging Rules and, 5-7
　　Newspaper Cataloging Manual, 5-7,24, 68
　　title variations, 23-24,26,27
　　uniform titles, 23-27
　Center for Research Libraries participation, 68-69
　CONSER program and, 4-5,6,8,9,68
　development, 3-4
　funding, 5,9
　guidelines, 7-9
　Library of Congress and, 4,5-6,7,8,68,69
　MARC format and, 4,5,9,68
　microcomputer use, 143-151
　non-extant titles and, 10

OCLC database and, 4,5,8,9,68,69
   microcomputer use and, 144,145,146,147,149
   National Endowment for the Humanities and, 3,4,7,8,9,68,150
   purpose, 3
University of Illinois, ethnic newspaper collection, 65
University of Minnesota, Immigration History Research Center, 69
Upton, Emory, 123
USA Today, index, 134
USMARC Format for Holdings Locations, 9

Velox files, in newspaper reference library, 79,80,90

Vertical file, in newspaper reference library, 80
Virgin Islands, United States Newspaper Program bibliographic grant, 8
VU/TEXT, 139,140

Wall Street Journal, index, 2,135,136,137
Washington Post, 122
   index, 136,138
Washington Times, 122
Western Reserve Historical Society, 8
Western Sun, 118
Wisconsin State Historical Society, 8
Wooding, Nathaniel, 115,116
Wordprocessing, 144-145,147-148,150,151

For Product Safety Concerns and Information please contact our EU
representative GPSR@taylorandfrancis.com
Taylor & Francis Verlag GmbH, Kaufingerstraße 24, 80331 München, Germany

www.ingramcontent.com/pod-product-compliance
Lightning Source LLC
Chambersburg PA
CBHW052126300426
44116CB00010B/1800